ROCK BOTTOM TO ROCK STAR

ROCK BOTTOM TO
ROCK STAR

LESSONS FROM THE BUSINESS
SCHOOL OF HARD KNOCKS

Ryan Blair

PORTFOLIO/PENGUIN

An imprint of Penguin Random House LLC
375 Hudson Street
New York, New York 10014

ISBN 9781101980552 (Hardcover)
ISBN 9781101980576 (eBook)

ROCK BOTTOM TO ROCK STAR is available at a discount when purchased in quantity for sales promotions or corporate use. Special editions, which include personalized covers, excerpts, and corporate imprints, can be created when purchased in large quantities. For more information, please call (212) 572-2232 or e-mail specialmarkets@penguinrandomhouse.com. Your local bookstore can also assist with discounted bulk purchases using the Penguin Random House corporate Business-to-Business program. For assistance in locating a participating retailer, e-mail B2B@penguinrandomhouse.com.

Printed in the United States of America
1   3   5   7   9   10   8   6   4   2

Set in Kepler Std with Knockout
Book design by Daniel Lagin

While the author has made every effort to provide accurate telephone numbers, Internet addresses, and other contact information at the time of publication, neither the publisher nor the author assumes any responsibility for errors, or for changes that occur after publication. Further, the publisher does not have any control over and does not assume any responsibility for author or third-party websites or their content.

AUTHOR'S NOTE

I would like to express my deepest gratitude for my biographer and writing partner of eight years, Shannon Constantine Logan, for extracting my innermost thoughts, deciphering my handwriting, and writing this book with me.

THIS BOOK CONTAINS POTTY MOUTH

You can't just bleep out colorful language in a book the way you can with a documentary, and unlike albums, books don't come with parental advisory ratings, so I struggled with whether or not to give you the uncensored version of my thinking process in my writing this time around. (I swear a lot more in my mind than I do in real life, rest assured.) After some debate, I decided that my readers could handle it. But if you're sensitive to strong language, then definitely consider bleeping out my f-bombs yourself. Also, out of respect for my mom, who is going to probably read this book, and because it may also be read in high schools, I've omitted a number of stories that were either too explicit for mass media or weren't relevant to business. If you want those stories, I've included them in the bonus content, which you can get by signing up for the newsletter on my website: ryanblair.com

One last note, I did my best to make sure all the facts and figures lined up in this book, but I did change some people's names for privacy purposes.

CONTENTS

CONTENTS

ROCK BOTTOM TO ROCK STAR

READ THIS FIRST

This isn't a rags-to-riches story, because not everyone comes from rags or wants riches. This book isn't about a charmed path to success or some untouchable fairy tale that nobody can relate to—this is about going from rock bottom to rock star, something that everybody can relate to. Can you relate?

Think about it. Everyone has had at least one rock-bottom moment: lost a job, landed in the hospital, went through a breakup, had to borrow money, repeated the cycle—because not one of us is immune to adversity. And everyone has had at least one "rock star" moment. Can you remember that one time you got recognized in class, or someone thanked you for your contribution to their life, or you looked back to see your pastor, mentor, or parents smiling at you with pride? You were a rock star, even for just one second. This book is about learning how to take those moments at the bottom, when you're beaten down, exhausted, embarrassed, and cornered, and using them to propel yourself forward, when you get to shine your brightest—and not just in your imagination, like when you were a kid and still believed you could be anything (even a rock star).

Today the term "rock star" has a whole new meaning; it isn't exclusive to someone on a stage holding a mic. You can be a rock star CEO, employee, or mom—a rock star is anybody who embodies the qualities of success and lives a life that lets them own their own stage. In the tech industry people always talk about the rock star engineer or the rock star coder. On the philanthropy side there are rock star fund-raisers (there are individuals out there raising more money than Bono, on a regular basis). There are rock star advertising execs. You don't need to be a millionaire to be a rock star; you don't need to quit your job. You can start wherever you are, in whatever industry or position you've already chosen. But you have to start now.

One of my friends, James Moorhead, is a great example of a rock star chief marketing officer. He created the brand campaign that reinvigorated Old Spice. Here's a man in his 30s who came up with a totally crazy idea—a half-man, half-horse spokesperson—for an aging brand at Proctor & Gamble with declining sales. Most people would hate working on a project that reminds them of their dad's cologne, but James was up for a challenge. He got a team together, came up with the ads and social media strategy, and launched it. The campaign went viral, he won prestigious awards (including an Emmy) for his concept, and Old Spice went from being in the gutter to being a top brand again.

This rock star marketer went on to become the chief marketing officer at DISH Network (and currently, Metromile). All of this happened because he believed it could, he committed to it, and took action.

I'm living the rock star life, a life that I created, one that I built with my own hands through countless battles. I've had ups and downs, but I've always strived to stay true to myself. I've started many companies over the course of my career and have been running ViSalus for the past twelve years, and even though my trajectory has been upward, that doesn't mean it's been easy. I've personally gone broke starting companies, had to sell companies and then buy them back. I planned an IPO (only to cancel it) and survived the 2008 recession. And in between, I wrote a *New York Times* best seller, made *Time* magazine's highest paid under 40 list (number five), collected trophies for my documentary, and was named Ernst & Young Entrepreneur of the Year, all while making tens of millions of dollars.

My rules for being a rock star are simple: Rule 1. Don't listen to the noise. Especially in this day and age, any fool with a mobile phone and a social media account thinks he's an expert, so don't listen to useless, negative messaging, and only take advice from those who are qualified to give it. Rule 2. Don't believe your own hype. The moment you start celebrating, you've left the stage. It wasn't celebration that made you a rock star, it was hard work. Remember that. Rule 3. Practice. There will be times where you're going to get rusty, and you're going to ask yourself, can I still do this? You have to get out there, play, rehearse, get feedback from your "audience," and modify your performance. Rule 4.

Surround yourself with the right musicians. You have to constantly assess the people you choose to hang with. Are they helping you move forward or are they just along for the ride? Are they building you up, or tearing you apart? I've lost relatives over this. Rule 5. Always remember where you came from.

I know not everyone reading this book is a rock star. If you don't have a rock star story yet, start with your rock bottom. Start from that place of fear and uncertainty, wherever you are at this moment. Maybe you've had enough, or maybe someone's had enough of you? Been fired? Got passed up for the big promotion again? Or maybe you're just tired of seeing rock stars all around you while you're still just scraping by. One of the reasons I wrote *Nothing to Lose, Everything to Gain*, and talk openly about my fucked-up upbringing, is because my ultimate rock-bottom moment—going to jail—is what made me who I am. Prior to writing my first book, I used to wear long sleeves to hide my gang tattoos during business meetings. Now I'm comfortable showing my scars. Don't forget your rock-bottom moments, and don't be ashamed of them. Some may criticize you, but there are also a lot of people out there who will relate to your story. Your story is an asset, and every time you tell it to someone, not only are you giving them hope, you're one step further away from rock bottom.

What you'll find in this book are stories from my own life—the highs and lows—intended to give you a feeling for the rhythm of entrepreneurship and inspire you. For the times when I hit bottom, I've included what I've learned, and specific instructions about how I got through them. For the times when I found myself living the rock star life, I talk about how to avoid my mistakes and not blow your success. In *Nothing to Lose*, I wrote about my earlier years in business, what I learned, and how I demanded success, with everything to gain. Now I'm writing from the standpoint of having achieved success, with everything to lose, and talking about how life can send us from the top to the bottom again to start all over, wiser and stronger. In my first book, I told you how I did it; in *Rock Bottom to Rock Star*, I will show you how you can do it, too.

Now read the book and go create your own multiplatinum career.

CHAPTER I
BE A BOSS

I t's hard to be a boss if you're at rock bottom. If you're like me you're probably thinking, "Where do I start?" Whether you're looking for work right now, changing careers, or have spent many years in an industry, the only way you'll become a rock star anything is to start taking responsibility for your life—be the boss of it.

My stepfather had a saying: "Do more than what you get paid for, and you'll always get paid more." What that meant to me was that if you're doing more than what you're getting paid for, your bosses will likely notice it, and you'll get a raise. If they don't notice you going above and beyond your job, you'll leave, and the next company you work for will give you more. In other words, you need to take control of your career. That's what I mean by being a boss. Don't wait for others to give you structure or provide the path. Take what you already have and expand on it—add more value than they expect—and as a result, you'll become even more valuable. This formula applies to everything. The more value you add today the more value you'll receive later.

Before Bruce Springsteen was a rock star, he would play small club gigs—these were less than desirable venues—and he took on the task of collecting the band's nightly pay and distributing it among his bandmates. That's how he got the nickname "The Boss."

When I say "be a boss," I am not only speaking to entrepreneurs like myself, but also to employees, parents, teachers, engineers, artists—really anyone who is focused on taking their game to the next level. There are different types of bosses in the business world, but all the good ones have these three things in common: they take responsibility, they add value to everything they do, and they own their careers. So, my question to you is: what are *you* going to do to earn the nickname "The Boss" as you seek to become a rock star in your chosen field?

Learn the Rules to Break Them

Most people are held back by the belief that there are smarter, better qualified, better connected people already in line ahead of them, so they don't take their shot, or, worst case, they sit back and wait for a turn that may never come.

There's an old Steve Jobs documentary that inspired me at a

young age, and in it he was interviewed after he was ousted from Apple. In the interview he said, "Everything around you, everything about this thing you call life, was made up by people no smarter than you."

We are given so many hard-and-fast rules about life: Save your money instead of investing it. You have to go to college to get a good job. It takes money to make money. And if you work forty hours a week for forty years, you can retire happily ever after. These are just some of the rules that are imposed on us by our parents, our teachers, and our well-meaning friends, and many times as we make our way through life, we find out that the rules set by others don't always apply. People create rules based on their respective belief systems. And people's belief systems, most of the time, come from their parents or from their specific environments. So, it's impossible that your belief system will completely match anyone else's.

If a rule doesn't work for you, you should question it. The rules were written by people, people no smarter than you.

One of my earliest mentors, Fred Warren, used to laugh at me whenever I would argue with him. He'd say, "What I like about you, Ryan, is that you'd rather beg for forgiveness than ask for permission." In *Nothing to Lose* I mention that he would tell me that he "broke his pick on me." To me that meant that I wouldn't compromise. You might not like some of my stories or agree with all of my philosophies, and you might even hate everything I stand for—who I am, the wealth I've acquired, the person I was in the past—but there is no question that I learned the hard way, and I earned the hard way. Don't compromise or let people who don't share your values convince you to do what *they* think is right. Everybody has their own set of rules, and their rules don't need to rule you.

My goal with this book isn't to force my rules onto you, it's to help you see some of the rules at play, so that you can find the ones you agree with—and break the ones you don't. We have a choice—we can follow others' rules, or we can find our own truth, but either way, we have to be aware.

Like Picasso said, "Learn the rules like a pro, so you can break them like an artist."

Business School of Hard Knocks

I started college while I was still on probation. I got my only "degree" on the streets from the School of Hard Knocks. And even though I didn't have a high school diploma, I had already done business—but none of it was legal. My stepfather's rules were nonnegotiable: never steal, get a job, go to school, and no girls allowed in my room. The alternatives—jail or going back to my old neighborhood—weren't really an option. I reluctantly enrolled at Moorpark Community College. My first semester I failed, I got nearly all Fs. This wasn't going to help me keep my room and board. I had to come up with a plan.

Every morning I'd drive my 1978 Toyota Corolla (with wood paneling on the sides) to school while listening to audiotapes on various subjects I was interested in, such as vocabulary (because

I didn't have one), or listening to recordings of my teachers' lectures. I recorded everything because that was how I learned best; I figured out that I had a gift, when I focused, for retaining what I heard. And focused I was. My addiction to being smart had started.

One day I got to my humanities class a little early, and what do you do when you're a twenty-year-old kid? I was pacing the halls reading the bulletin boards on the walls. The first one was some public health and safety announcement, then upcoming events on campus, and the third bulletin was the dean's list. I thought, *Why even bother reading the dean's list, it's not like I know anyone on here.* But I had ten more minutes to kill, so I scanned the A's, the B's . . . and there was the name Blair. *Wait, is there someone else named Ryan Blair on campus here? That's interesting.* Then it settled in: *That's me!* At that point I started reverse engineering the process: *What did I do to make that list?* With my remaining five minutes to kill, I went directly to the administration building so they could confirm that it was me, and not a typo. I felt like a genuine rock star. (I had made many "lists" before, and I was not proud of any of them.) I had gone farther than I'd thought possible; from the "D" list to the dean's list. It was time to spike the mic.

With my first taste of academic accomplishment, I got accepted to California Lutheran University, and transferred over to their business school as a sophomore. I was able to get student loans and grants by applying for affirmative action status, which was possible because my guardians were the state of California (I was made a ward of the court at the age of fourteen) and because my address had once been 380 North Hillmont, Ventura—Juvenile Hall.

When you're poor, you learn to leverage your environment, or be leveraged by it. These survival skills have gotten me through every economic phase of my life. On my first day on campus at Cal Lutheran, I signed up for a credit card and got approved. Then I signed up for another, and another. I saw the age of the Internet coming, and I saw my opportunity to join it. I started borrowing money off my credit cards and using my student loans to trade high-flying Internet stocks during the dotcom boom. This wasn't easy. I still had a full course load, and I would ambitiously wake up at (or stay up until) 5 a.m. every morning to do my research and to make my trades before classes started. I was getting an excellent education, learning fractions and finance, on top of my other studies. (Prior to college, I never passed a math class, but I could count money. It turns out counting money is what counts in business.)

At twenty years old I was making around $130,000 a year, while in school, trading stocks. (Adjusted for inflation, it was the equivalent of $200,000 a year.) School was hard for me, but making money came naturally, especially back then, when credit was flowing and technology stocks were riding high on the rising tide of the Internet. It was easy to win.

I got a job fixing and testing computers in a data center, while I day-traded and went to college. It still wasn't enough for me. I wanted more. I had watched my father lose everything trying to stay in the middle class. I saw the middle class as a compromise and a trap—an economic strategy set by the rich—and I had sworn I'd rather be poor than land in the middle.

I bought my first house at the age of 21 for $165,000 with no money down, and negotiated cash back. With the money I got, you can guess what came next—I invested it. While my friends were in college trying to keep up with each other, I was doing the exact opposite of what I watched my father do with his life. He bought brand-new cars to show off or plunged his money into drugs and other superficial diversions. I lived cheaply so I could invest even more. I drank Folgers instant coffee instead of Starbucks and ate chicken-and-rice bowls from Costco—for a couple bucks each. I lived on $10 a day when I was making $350 a day, and I dreamed of making $1,000 a day (or someday $10,000 a day). I watched people no smarter than me making their own rules and their fortunes, and I believed I could do it, too.

The beautiful thing about skills is that they can be learned, and the great thing about experience is that it's earned. I knew how to survive, and I had figured out how to make money on the streets. So, now all I had to do was to learn about business. I knew the only way I would be able to learn business quickly, and apply what I had learned academically, was to practice it. My instincts were to start a company.

When I worked at the day center at Logix, back then computers would break down constantly (these were the Novell days). We literally had people on call 24 hours a day, seven days a week, just in case. I'd get woken up at all hours of the night with emergency calls from junior technicians, and I'd have to go into the office at 3 a.m. sometimes just to watch the server index for hours, swap out a motherboard, or reboot a system. It dawned on me that if my company was going through this, then other companies must be, too. And not all of them had staff on call 24/7. The idea for my first company was born, a computer repair service called 24x7 Tech (When your computer is a wreck, call 1-800-24x7-Tech!), which led me to start my next company, Sky-Pipeline. Soon, I found myself facing a big decision: Do I leave school and risk it all to try to become a rock star entrepreneur like other college dropouts (e.g., Dell, Gates, etc.)? Or do I stay in school and finish what I had started? (Something no one in my family had ever done.)

The question kept me up at night. I had come so far, so much further than anyone else in my family. I was firmly in the middle class, making more money than my father ever had, and if I left college now, it could destroy my middle-class status. *But what does a college degree matter if you're a millionaire?* I thought. Then again, if I wanted a career in corporate America, and to keep that cushy six-figure salary, the smartest thing to do was to stay in college.

I sought out the best advice I could get. I decided to ask my mom.

When I approached my mother, I had been up for twenty-four hours straight, trading stocks, handling my new company's operations, and doing homework. I had bags under my blood-shot eyes, and I was afraid she was going to think I was crazy. I had lost so many friends once my business started taking off, and even some of my own family had reacted with jealousy. She was one of the few who knew the person I had become, and she was unconditionally proud of me.

I told her, "I'm leaving school to work on my company full time." (I know, not the best way to request advice from your mother.)

I'll never forget her face. First she looked confused, then she said, "Are you kidding me? You make more than your father ever did, you're on the dean's list, you just got into a private school, you're only twenty years old, and you are really taking for granted how lucky you are."

Now, I'm a self-proclaimed mama's boy, but those were not the words I was trying to hear. And I was exhausted.

"First of all, I don't believe in luck," I said. "Second, Bill Gates left school, Steve Jobs, Craig McCaw—"

"You're not *Bill Jobs*, Ryan," she said.

At that point I realized I couldn't win a debate with my mother on this topic. When it came to the subject of her son, she was the expert. I stopped talking about it with her, but my inner monologue didn't stop. *I will show her that I am going to make it. And I'm going to make it big. I'll make her proud.*

After I relaxed a bit, I realized that maybe my mom wasn't the best person to seek advice from about this. I was asking business advice from someone who didn't know anything about it. So, I went to the dean of the Cal Lutheran business school, Dr. Harry Domicone, and asked for his counsel.

He said, "Ryan, my job is to keep you in school, so we get

tuition, but in your case you'll be back here keynoting to the graduating class someday anyway, so leave, run your business, and come back if you need to, or when we invite you."

When I compared his words to my mother's, I recognized her fears as my own. I decided I wouldn't let fear stop me. I left college heading into my senior year. But the decision took its toll on me psychologically. To this day, whenever I'm debating a tough decision, I still have nightmares about deciding whether to leave school.

College isn't just where you learn many of the rules. Right now, going to college *is* the rule. The lessons I learned in college were priceless, but so were those I learned from practice. In school I learned how to count to a billion, I learned marketing, and I learned about how the business world would one day become globalized. From practice, I learned to apply what college had given me, but I also learned, by failing, how not to fear failure; figured out how my self-esteem worked; and discovered ways to get around my learning disabilities. I started educating myself, using influence, ambition, and making connections to further my career, and I learned to leverage my brand—tattoos and all. And most important, I learned that the world is run by entrepreneurs and rock stars.

There's More Than One Path

According to a recent article in the *New York Times*, 14 percent of Google's current workforce doesn't have a college degree.

Proof that many of us didn't take the prescribed route, yet we can still offer a special kind of ingenuity and creativity to the companies we lead and work for. One of the five largest companies in the world has recognized this, and there's something to be learned by it.

My teachers at continuation high school had a favorite pastime: basking in their tenure and fantasizing about their retirement. I vividly remember Mr. Conner bragging loudly about the fact that the school couldn't fire him and talking about the summer to come, when he would get to live carefree for three months straight. Conner, and the other teachers like him, would say things like, "If you don't get good grades, graduate, go to college, and get a good job, you'll never own a home."

My stepfather, Bob Hunt, didn't buy into anyone else's rules but his own, and when I'd come home from school and project my teachers' beliefs onto him, he'd immediately correct me and say with a smirk on his face, "Bullshit... You don't need a diploma to buy a house. There's nowhere on a mortgage application that asks you if you graduated from college."

Think about how many people in our society, even today, believe they won't be able to buy a house if they don't go to college or have a degree. I'm not saying that college isn't the best path to get you where you are going, I'm just saying that it's not the *only* path. Everyone who goes to school comes out with a plan, but not necessarily a profession.

I've obviously chosen a different way. I left college to start a company. If you're reading this book, you've likely chosen a different way as well, or you're on a path that was chosen for you by someone else and you're looking to get off it. For those of you reading this who did put thousands of hours and hundreds of thousands into your college degree, you may be realizing by now that hard work doesn't always pay off.

Hard Work Doesn't Always Pay Off

I worked my ass off in my twenties, with school, work, and my start-up. I had no time for a social life. If most employees work 2,080 hours a year (forty hours a week), I more than doubled that. I'd work an average of sixteen hours a day, six or seven days a week, which is about 4,992 hours a year. After a hundred days in a row of this, I'd get burned out, take a few days off, and then go back to my regimen. My logic was: *I'm working so hard. I should be rich someday.* Of course, anyone who works their ass off in our society knows that that's not how it works.

Justine Musk, the first wife of billionaire Elon Musk (CEO of Tesla Motors and founder of PayPal), recently offered some advice to a Quora.com reader who asked: "Will I become a billionaire if I am determined to be one and put in all the necessary work required?"

Her answer was, essentially, no.

This excerpt from her response was priceless:

> *The world doesn't throw a billion dollars at a person because the person wants it or works so hard they feel they*

deserve it. (The world does not care what you want or de-
serve.) The world gives you money in exchange for something
it perceives to be of equal or greater value: something that
transforms an aspect of the culture, reworks a familiar story
or introduces a new one, alters the way people think about
the category, and make use of it in daily life. There is no
roadmap, no blueprint for this . . .

I still work sixteen-hour days—that's one rule that hasn't
changed. Hard work is mandatory if you want to become a millionaire, multimillionaire, or a billionaire. But instead of ex-
hausting myself, making other people rich, I invest my energy
exactly the way Justine Musk talked about: into companies that
create solutions to society's problems—and the bigger the problems I solve, the more money I make.

The Competition Is You

In early 2013, I was relaxing in my $12,000 British Airways first-
class seat, on my way to meet a woman I was dating at the
time—one of the most beautiful and intelligent human beings I
had ever met, and one of the world's top financial experts. At
that time, I was the fifth highest paid person under 40 in all of
Wall Street (yes, I'm mentioning this again, forgive me, I'm competitive); however, just as the Quora.com reader asked Ms. Musk,
I often asked myself: *When will I be a billionaire?*

I read a lot, especially on flights, and I had just cracked open the *Fortune* magazine "40 Under 40" issue, the one that featured Marissa Mayer, the CEO of Yahoo. At the time I was 36 (she was a year or two older than me). I started reading the list—number one, two, three, four, five, six, seven, eight—and suddenly I thought, *Why am I not on this list?*

I didn't make the list, but I could have been among those individuals. I had no excuse. The only reason I wasn't on that list was because of me. I was so pissed, I got out my journal and wrote myself a letter:

Why I'm not on the Forbes 40 Under 40 List!

I sought good times rather than excellence.

I wanted to go out and have fun and travel the world and party rather than prove to myself I could build something on a world scale.

I am busy celebrating my victories as opposed to creating new ones.

I am undisciplined and I'm not the only person I'm hurting.

The competition is Me.

And my opponent is winning.

I tend to see everything in life as a competition. First I thought I was competing with my dad. I wanted to be a better man than he was and prove that I didn't need him. Then it was my stepdad, a smart and successful real estate entrepreneur—I wanted to make more money than he did. Then I competed with other companies in my industry. I was even subconsciously competing with the girlfriend I was flying to London to spend time with.

That wasn't a rock-bottom moment I was having on that flight; it was a "wake the fuck up" moment. The truth is, I am my own competition. Going from nothing to being worth $70 million in seven years wasn't enough because my greatest asset, my true potential, hadn't been reached. The bottom line is, I may not make the 40 Under 40 list, but I plan to hit some lists in the near future. No excuses.

The Excuse Department Is Closed

Long before I was considered one of the highest-paid executives in America, I was sitting in my office in Mid-Wilshire in Los Angeles. It was late 2009, during the middle of the Great Recession, and we had just laid off a bunch of people. The wing where my office was located had once housed thirty PathConnect employees—the people who'd helped me create the first social networking site for goal-setting—and now it was just me. Occasionally I would go over to the other side of the fourteenth floor where all the ViSalus employees were, but it was clear that I wasn't welcome. I was by title the CEO of ViSalus, but our parent company, Blyth, Inc., had embedded their consultants so deep in the organization that it was clear that I no longer had the jurisdiction I once did.

Every morning I would walk through the ghost town of empty desks, go into my corner office, and shut the door. I was still taking calls, but I made myself as busy as possible. If someone wanted to meet with me they had to make an appointment first, because that's the way I could hide.

That day, a ViSalus promoter, someone who had been with us for quite a while, called me up. He was having difficulties, the same difficulties that most of our distributors were experiencing during the recession: sales were going down and there was a lack of resources. Essentially, GJ Reynolds had called me up to complain, and I heard him give me excuse after excuse for why he wasn't selling. He said, "If we only had super glossy collateral . . . If we only had a better DVD . . . more products . . . new countries . . . more commissions . . ."

Actually, the data I had sitting on my desk in late 2009 indicated that we were starting to see some green shoots, finally: We had just launched the Body by Vi Challenge, and a few of our promoters were having moderate success with it. None of us knew it at the time, but those green shoots would turn into a harvest that we would eventually use to rise up out of our economic death spiral. But for the moment, all I could see was slight progress, and I was doing my best to filter the barrage of negativity coming at me over the phone.

As an entrepreneur it's hard to be straight with stakeholders. You don't want to tell them, "Listen, the God's honest truth is that there's no cash in the bank." You scare them like that. So, at first I tried placating him. I kept saying, "I hear you." But the excuses continued. For every positive thing I said, GJ would follow it up with a "but."

He just wouldn't stop. Finally, I took a deep breath. Here I was: I had lost all my money, millions of dollars; I had a newborn son; Blyth was staging a coup and attempting to fire me; there was conflict between me and my cofounders, and my original employees had all been turned against me; and I'm listening to this guy complain that he can't do his job because there's a spelling error on the Web site. *I am trying to save my company and not go bankrupt and he's worried about the Web site? Fuck this guy.*

"GJ, this is unfortunate," I said abruptly. "I've kept this from you, but there've been a lot of layoffs in the company."

GJ stopped his litany for a moment and listened.

"I've had to lay off longtime employees, good friends, and most of the staff," I continued. "In fact, we had to let go of an entire department."

"What department?" GJ asked.

"It's called the Excuse Department," I said.

There was a long pause on the phone, and then I heard GJ laughing. He thought it was very funny.

"But—" he said.

I immediately cut him off. "They're gone, GJ," I said. "There's no one left to take your excuses anymore. Sorry."

Then I slammed that phone down as hard as I could in a very "I don't give a fuck" kind of way. Thankfully, GJ had a thick skin and he knew I meant the best for both of us. We went on to have a great working relationship. But from that point on, anytime anyone gave me an excuse, I told them, "Times are tough—I've laid off the Excuse Department. There's no one here to listen to your excuse."

If you want to be a successful entrepreneur, you can't make excuses, and you sure as hell can't take them. There will always be an excuse for not doing work, for not trying a little harder, for not starting a company, for not finishing this book—in fact, there are more excuses for not doing something than there are reasons for doing it. To be a boss, you have to start thinking like a boss. You have to stop yourself from making excuses, and to stop others, too.

I was having Chinese food with my friend Gerard Adams the other night and he explained to me the game of adding the words "in bed" to the end of the fortune in the cookie. It's hilarious: "Success lies in the hands of those who want it *in bed*," and it works. I want you to make your "fortune" in business, so just like the fortune cookie game, I want to play a new game with you called "like a boss." I want you to add "like a boss" to the end of each sentence about everything you do: "I showed up to that meeting *like a boss*," or "I got my son fed, dressed, and off to school by 7 a.m. *like a boss*." Whether it's reading this book, pitching an investor, shaking someone's hand, going to law school, or picking up your kids from soccer practice—do it like a boss. And don't make or take excuses from anyone, expecially not yourself.

CHAPTER 2
QUIT DIGGING

L ooking down from my balcony at the Marina City Club, I counted the floors below. There were fourteen stories between me and the pavement. *I'm just going to fucking jump.*

It was 2004, and I was forced to file for bankruptcy. I had gone through a divorce, sold my first two companies, and blew all the money I had made trying to live the life of a rock star without having the net worth to support it. I was living in a condo that I rented from my stepfather, and I couldn't even pay him the rent. I didn't know what I was going to do next, or how I was going to find the money I needed to survive. I had a $100,000 sports car in the garage that I hated every time I drove it because I didn't have enough money left in my account to fill up the gas tank all the way. My mailbox was so full of urgent notices from bill collectors that I stopped bothering to open the mail. I pushed my family and my friends away. Soon everyone would know that I had blown it, and that I had failed. *What does it matter if I jump? My life is already over.*

I stood looking at the pavement below me. The moment passed. I had lost friends to suicide and I knew it was a selfish act, one that hurts everyone who loves you. I was being selfish for even thinking such a thought. *How could I do that to my mother and my sisters?* It dawned on me that I should be more grateful for what I had versus what I didn't have. I walked back inside and shut the sliding glass door behind me.

I would have to pull myself out of the hole, somehow.

The Hustle

I came up with an idea: I'd put an ad on craigslist, and hire a person to call around and book speaking gigs for me. I had a story to tell. If there was one thing I knew how to do, it was sell myself. This would be the hustle of a lifetime.

My formula for keeping my head above water was simple—if I hired an employee today, and I had to pay them every two weeks, then I had two weeks to make enough to pay them, or I wouldn't eat. It was risky; I'd never hire people for a job and not be able to pay them, so avoiding this outcome gave me the motivation I needed.

Almost immediately we got traction. I worked on my public-speaking skills by teaching entrepreneurship at local high schools. The kids were learning and so was I. I taught sales seminars for free to salespeople at real estate offices, car dealerships, and anywhere else they would let me through the door. At the end of my presentation, when they asked for more, I would sell them that "more"—more of me. They got tickets to hear a longer lecture on sales techniques that would take their incomes to the next level.

There I was, showing up to my speaking gigs in my sports car, wearing a suit and tie, telling others how to start a business or be a great salesman when, on some days, I had to take loose change to the change machines at the supermarket just to get enough cash to put $20 in my gas tank without embarrassing myself, and then pray I had enough gas in my car to make it to the next appointment where, hopefully, I'd make a sale. I only ate what I killed, and that's it.

I know what you're probably thinking: "How can you talk to anyone about becoming successful when you're broke?" The answer is simple; in my mind, I *was* a success. I knew how to become successful—after all, I had made millions, mostly for others—I just didn't know how to *keep* my success. And I wasn't teaching people how to keep their money, just how to make it.

At the end of the first two weeks, I paid my employees and had just enough left for food. I knew if I could get this business model going, eventually I'd have money for me. But it was going to take more than just delivering free speeches; I had to get creative.

It turned out that the guy I hired from craigslist, a man named John Laun, would be my first real ally. He was an English major at UCLA, sarcastic and funny, like the screenplays he wrote. One day John and I were talking about how much we loved Chipotle and I jokingly told him to call up Chipotle and ask them to sponsor me. Why not? Of course, we were looking for money, and of course they said no, but John got them to give us an in-kind donation instead: free meal coupons that I handed out at the high schools where I spoke. But I also kept a lot of them for myself. At one point I realized I had eaten Chipotle every single day for six months. I had even taken a few girls out on dates there and paid for our meals with coupons. I called this period my "Chipotle Days." A few good things came out of this time. John Laun turned out to be one of my loyal team members; he's still employed at ViSalus, and he's now a millionaire as a result of the stock he got in the company. I also got a powerful lesson that "your next meal is only a phone call away," and I still love Chipotle to this day, just not the Chipotle Days.

Shortly after the Chipotle Days, which lasted for about a year, the company that bought my second company, SkyPipeline, sold to Covad, a large broadband and data communications company. That meant the SkyPipeline stock I had was liquid, and suddenly, I had a few hundred thousand dollars' worth of breathing room. I met two entrepreneurs, Nick Sarnicola and Blake Mallen, and we started ViSalus in 2005. But I still didn't have any real money. I was bouncing around from office to office all over Los Angeles, giving four to six speeches a day. I'd sell enough tickets to my big seminar to book a venue, and pull in just enough cash to get by and keep my start-up hopes alive. There was nothing fun about it; it was a fucking grind.

One of my longtime close friends literally called everyone we knew to talk shit, and called me a false prophet. Even my family mocked me. They joked that I was raised a "poor black child," a quote from Steve Martin from the movie *The Jerk*, and said things like "fake it till you make it." It got so bad that at my sister's birthday dinner, my eight-year-old niece chimed in, reciting the movie quote, while everyone laughed. I lost my temper. I told my family I wasn't a joke and I wouldn't be part of a family that didn't respect me. I grabbed the bill, paid for it, said, "You're welcome," and left.

The Rule of Holes

"Rock bottom" is often used to describe the very bottom of a fall; sometimes it takes a long time to get there, and sometimes it happens in a flash. Picture the ground giving way beneath you—you're hanging on to whatever you can, but each move you make somehow triggers another sharp downward plunge. Sometimes you find stable footing temporarily, just to find that it crumbles away under the weight of events or decisions you've made—decisions that may be unrelated to the one that caused you to fall in the first place. You only know a true rock-bottom moment when you're sitting on that concrete, nothing left to lose, and you're ready to devise a "concrete" plan to stop falling, swearing to yourself you'll never be in that place again. It's a moment of clarity like no other.

Fred Warren, a venture capitalist and one of my mentors, once said to me, "When you find yourself in a hole, quit digging."

There's always going to be a mixture of shame, grief, self-pity, and anger when you hit bottom. It could have been your own stupid decisions, a bad investment, the economy, an investor, or someone who screwed you. There's a long list of things, both within and outside of your control, that led you into that hole—either way, there is only one way out of a hole: Quit digging.

The most important thing to realize when you've hit bottom is that it's temporary. You're not going to die; it just feels that way. You've failed. Life is over. Everyone thinks you're a fraud, and your asshole friends and family are going to rub it in your face or, worse, talk behind your back. This is all momentary, issues that will last one month, or three months, or a year, but if you look at the trajectory of your entrepreneurial career over ten, twenty, or thirty years, hitting bottom is just a blip. Everyone is going to have moments of intense dissatisfaction. If you spend a lot of time and energy on those mistakes, you'll never get yourself out of the hole. And all those nay-saying friends? Don't worry, you'll prove them wrong one day.

This is the first rule of holes: When you're at the bottom, you have to quit digging. There's no time to question it. Stop asking questions like, "How did I get here? I'm a good guy, why did this happen to me?" You're just shoveling deeper and deeper. It's time to fight! And get yourself out of that hole. Apathy and self-pity are going to be your enemies in this struggle. You have to self-motivate even under the most extreme circumstances. Then you have two options: You can either find someone or something to prove wrong (to prove yourself right) or you can make a vow you'll never go back to that dark place. You have to take responsibility for where you are in life, no matter where you find yourself, whether it's flying on a private jet, dead broke, or rummaging in your couch cushions for change to fill your gas tank. You have to have tough conversations with yourself, and learn to fight your way out of your own holes.

Smiles and Cries

One of my least favorite business catchphrases is "hockey stick growth"—a sharp rise in data points on a chart after a long flat period—but if you look at my timeline, starting with nothing and progressing to the assets I have today, it looks exactly like that: a hockey stick. I want you to be aware of the "hockey sticks" in your own timelines, because this is exactly what most entrepreneurs' trajectories look like.

Early in my career I wrote software for the commodities industry. We'd write algorithms to trade on, then we'd go back over the data we had on all transactions and ask, If I tried this approach, would I feel like jumping off a cliff in the low periods? Would I be tempted to change my game plan in the highs?

One of the theories I had at that time was that if Friday's sales volume was low and the prices were down, people would think about the purchase over the weekend and they would buy on Monday. So, my simple algorithm was called "Buy Monday." I ran the algorithm and then went back and looked at all trades over twenty years. I realized that if I applied this to the back data for the last twenty years, overall I would have been up hundreds of percentages—but in one scenario, I would have lost money for fifty-two weeks in a row. That's a hell of a hockey stick handle. My question was, Would I have been able to psychologically withstand that long down period, in order to win over time? My answer was no. If you lose fifty-two weeks in a row, you'll start to doubt yourself, especially when you see your bank account drained, and you'll change the plan. But that's the wrong answer. In our everyday lives, we don't have control over how long the low points are going to last. I should have been psychologically prepared to withstand fifty-two weeks of loss, trusting that I would win in the end, but my relationship with money involves a lot of psychology that only I understand.

It seems like there should be a big difference between rock bottom and rock star, but there really isn't—in either scenario you want success. Rather, it's about finding something you believe in enough that you'll continue doing it even when success seems more than fifty-two weeks away.

When you look at your timeline, look at it the same way: There are long flat periods and sharp upswings, sometimes followed by prolonged declining periods. So, when you are considering your timeline's future, ask yourself if your strategy is based on your past results. Are you deploying a strategy that won't let you withstand a dry spell? Do you have enough in your bank account to weather it?

With ViSalus, knowing my industry and its cycles and having studied my competitors' data (just as I had when I was a young engineer writing trading algorithms), I knew I had to prepare myself for an inevitable down cycle—a long losing streak. Over the lifespan of my company, we've seen lots of "hockey sticks"—everything from near bankruptcy to being one of the fastest-growing companies in our sector to preparing for a total rebuild. The reason we're still standing today is I've somehow been able to withstand the losing streaks, and not lose myself completely in the winning streaks.

In the movie *Training Day*, Ethan Hawke's character, Jake Hoyt, tells Roger (played by Scott Glenn) that the streets are "all about smiles and cries." That's true in business, too. Your timeline will be filled with smiles and cries. Ultimately, success will be determined by whether or not you have the right psychology to control them.

CHAPTER 3

PAY ATTENTION TO YOUR TIME . . . LINE

get asked this question all the time: Knowing what you know now, *what would you tell your younger self?* My answer: Pay attention to your time . . . line. Your time is what you do today, this weekend, this month, and your timeline is the accumulation of what you've done for many years. The things I'm making real money on today, I started working on many years ago.

For instance, I started my real estate career as a "boy Friday" for my stepfather in 1996, and today I am making millions in real estate. When I was a teenager, I became obsessed with computers; in 2008 I created a piece of software that did $70 million in revenue for our company. Today, I invest in software start-ups. The first time I tried my hand at public speaking I was about twenty-five and there were no more than ten people in the room;

in 2012, I spoke to eighteen thousand people in a sold-out American Airlines Arena.

Get the point? What you do with your time today makes a big difference down the road. So, pay attention.

I used to be a sports fanatic. I would watch every NFL game, every NBA game. Football, soccer, tennis—I'd watch any sport out there, and I'd have my fair share of drinks while I was at it. That's the middle-class pastime, and that was my thing. One day, when I was about twenty-one, I asked myself, *How is this going to make me rich?* The answer was: It's not. Not unless I plan to own a sports team.

Today, I've all but dropped sports. I know that when I invest my time watching all these games, I'm making someone else rich. Time is a nonrenewable resource; once a moment is gone, it's gone forever. As a successful businessperson, you'll have to carefully examine your hobbies, your obligations, your pastimes, and all your other preoccupations to isolate the ones that waste time and pull you away from your business. Ideally, you're going to completely change the way you look at the twenty-four-hour clock and live nearly 100 percent of it intentionally.

For example, I *don't* waste my weekends watching sports, but I still love football, so I throw a Super Bowl party. I invite a variety of current and potential business partners, and we have a great time. Many times, I'll put a bucket at the door so everyone can drop cash into it; after the game, we donate the money to a charity. That way, I'm mixing business with pleasure, and I've enhanced both my life and my business.

Maybe you're a golfaholic—you can afford to play golf three

times a week, but you're stuck in the middle class. Unless you're really utilizing the networking benefits of rubbing elbows with investors and clients on the green, drop the golf altogether and make a promise to yourself that you'll pick it up again once you are wealthy.

Watching television or voraciously reading novels is the same time waste. You don't have to give up those things; you just have to adjust the way you spend your time so that you can focus on things that will help your business in some way. If you want to read, read for profit. You like movies? Watch a movie that will give you a new perspective on your career or inspire you. I read news articles, business books, and motivational stories. If you want to watch TV, choose a documentary or a film that piques your creativity. It's all about living with intentionality. There is a way to shape everything in life so that it serves you and drives you toward success.

One life-hack I recently made was to work out while I work. An exercise bike is perfect for that; I'll read or send e-mails or make calls while pedaling. A treadmill is a little less desirable because it's harder to send out a coherent e-mail when you're running, but you can certainly listen to an audiobook while running. Sometimes, the gym doesn't inspire me, so I'll go for a hike, and that helps me to clear my head. I also use hikes as an opportunity to interview prospective employees and entrepreneurs I'm considering investing with, or simply to talk with a colleague.

For instance, Lewis Howes reached out to me the other day and requested an interview. This is an author with one of the largest podcasts in the world right now (three million downloads a month), who frequently interviews business leaders, athletes, and other rock stars. Originally, we planned to do the interview over the phone, but the connection kept breaking up. Finally, Lewis said, "Hey, why don't I just come to you?"

I said, "Deal, but the meeting has to be at my house—after a hike."

Not only did we get a great interview that day, I felt like I got to know him. During the hike we became friends. Later, when he was writing *School of Greatness*, Howes contacted me again and we got a chance to talk about business. *Business Insider* even wrote an article about Howes and me working out together and how I use hiking as a tool to optimize my time.

The objective is to practice restraint, and to become intentional in all your actions. The more I grow as an entrepreneur and especially as a father, the less time I have to waste. I've been in every socioeconomic class in America—poor, middle class, and wealthy—and it's actually easier to be ambitious when you're living poor or paycheck-to-paycheck. You're in survival mode, and every second counts—you're likely not taking "staycations" every other week or taking off an entire afternoon to watch football. You have to grind it out. You have to hustle.

The point is that no matter which class you're starting from—whether you're trying to figure out how to pay for your next meal or floating in the illusory comfort of the middle class—the sooner you start optimizing your time, the more successful you'll be, and the more time you'll have to spend doing whatever you want. Like a true rock star.

CHAPTER 4
FIND YOUR SUPERPOWER

Before I left school, when I was excelling academically, I asked for a meeting with one of my professors, Gerald Fate, who taught my Eastern philosophy class. He said to me, "Ryan, when I'm teaching the class, I always feel like I'm speaking directly to you because you're engaged. But there are some things about you that you need to focus on."

One of the things he mentioned was the way I dressed. Gerald told me to pick a style, whatever style I liked, and stick with it. It struck me, years later, that he was trying to tell me I needed to create a signature. Every rock star artist has a signature style. It might be the way they play the piano that sounds different from any other pianist, or the way they sign their name, or a color palette they always use, or their unique singing style.

The other day I was watching a show called Brilliant Ideas on

Bloomberg.com, where they profiled Xu Bing, a Chinese artist with an immediately recognizable signature style. Bing had spent his entire career creating and playing with languages. He had invented four thousand new (and intentionally illegible) Chinese characters for a massive installation that launched his art career, designed ideograms using English alphabet calligraphy, and "wrote" a book made entirely of emojis, universal symbols that can be read by anyone in the world, regardless of their native language. This highly successful rock star artist had a desire to change the Chinese language, and he took the seed of that passion and turned it into a signature style that is different from any other artist's. He turned this into an art career, and as a result, I'm watching a documentary about him halfway around the world.

To be a rock star you must figure out what makes your work unique, nail this style, and hone it into a signature that clearly sets you apart from your peers. The world celebrates difference—project your difference.

I used to wear suits to work every day, until I realized that a suit wasn't my signature look. Now I rock a standard T-shirt, jeans, and a pair of Converse because this is the most comfortable outfit for me (especially when I have "decision fatigue"). I never dreamed that I'd be on stages speaking in front of hundreds of thousands of people either. The change was a side effect of telling my story, once I figured out that my story was part of my signature, my brand. I was actually extremely shy and battled stage fright for many years as I perfected myself on stage. I didn't start out knowing much about book publishing either, but

I had to communicate my story in a way that reached more people than could fit inside an auditorium. I committed to the idea of writing a book even before I knew my writing style. I worked with best-selling authors, editors, and writers, and I learned to write. Now I'm on my second book, and I'm still developing my individual writing style, but I know my voice. Being an author has turned into a big part of my brand.

Every time you see Mark Zuckerberg in his hoodie and jeans, he is communicating the story of his brand to you. Every time Madonna gives a flawless performance, she's communicating her signature style of perfectionism. We may not be as famous as Madonna, or as wealthy as Mark Zuckerberg, but everyone who is reading this book should be thinking about capturing their individual style and signature, perfecting their art or their instrument of choice, committing to it, and turning it into a rock star brand.

Stare Down

My son Reagan came home from school one day and told me that he was being bullied. He's a very sensitive boy, and has difficulty communicating, as many autistic kids do. If someone pushes him around, he really takes it hard. There's not a bone in him that wants to fight back, and yet he can't express his feelings, and that makes matters even worse. We all know how cruel boys can be to other little boys.

It reminded me of when I was a kid, and I told my dad I was being picked on at school. He said, "If anybody is mean to you, you punch him first, right in the face." And that's what I did. I pretty much punched my way through adolescence, and it got me nowhere in life except the principal's office. I got sent home from school so many times for fighting, I lost count. I would get suspended from school, but I'd never get punished at home for it. I'd walk in bloodied and bruised, and my father would just ask, "Did you win?"

My father's anger was something I learned to adapt to. He was a Vietnam vet with lingering trauma from his years in the service, and he taught me what he knew, which was how to fight. He told me fighting was the measure of a man. Years later, when my hatred got the best of me, it was my father's face I'd picture during a fight. But for a long time, I was speaking the only language I had in common with my father: violence. This became a major stumbling block in my life, and it wasn't until I had the strength to unclench my fists—literally and figuratively—that I was able to beat most any problem in life and business that came my way without having to resort to force.

So, when my son came home and said someone was picking on him, I thought about what I had been taught, and all the pain it had caused me in life, and then I thought about what John F. Kennedy was probably taught. Now, I have no idea what John F. Kennedy's dad, Joe Kennedy, actually taught his son, but in my idealized version of the Kennedy family, I was assuming that he didn't teach John to punch his adversaries in the face. Maybe he told him to be a diplomat and solve the issue without violence, or maybe he told him to be the bigger man and walk away, or to deal with bullies like a gentleman. Again, this was just a made-up standard that I had imagined, but it definitely served a purpose by helping me think about what advice to give my son.

I had an idea. I sat Reagan down and said, "You know, you have a superpower—a secret weapon. You can beat anyone in a staring contest."

Autistic kids don't often make eye contact; their reluctance has to do with the way their brains process visual information. But when they do, they can look right through you. Reagan can literally sit there for ten minutes, staring a hole into you, if he wants to. I've tried to mean-mug my son—to stare him down. I cannot win. He'll just smirk at me, with his blue eyes beaming (and mine blinking).

I told him, "Whenever someone messes with you, just use your secret weapon and tell them 'staring contest.'"

The next day at school, when the bully tried to pick on Reagan, he challenged him to a staring contest—and he won. Now my son walks around with more confidence, and anytime someone bullies him, he can use his superpower. He'll sit there for as long as he has to, but he will always win.

Reagan discovered his unique strength, and he can use it to his advantage to control situations and win confrontations in a way that doesn't require using his fists or telling the teacher. It's the same in business; every entrepreneur needs to find their own version of a staring contest, their own secret weapon. I used to know I could win a fight if I could throw the first punch. Now I know that nobody can become a successful entrepreneur by constantly getting into fights.

We all have to find our real sources of strength, and utilize them to the best of our ability. Every one of us has something that makes us unique—a strength. The key in business is to figure out what it is, develop it, and play that strength to the fullest.

When I was just starting my career, it was sales. That was my superpower. One time I was on a sales call and this veteran sales guy pulled me aside. He was in his sixties, and I was in my early twenties, and he stood so close to me I could smell his breath. I must have been rambling on, and he stopped me. He said, "You're one of the best salespeople in the world, but don't talk past the close ever again."

I got so much positive feedback about my abilities as a salesperson back then that I thought sales was my superpower. I learned to sell because it was my survival strategy. It turns out that I was in that room at that exact point in time, rubbing elbows with sales industry veterans, because I was not only a good salesman, but I was also thinking strategically. Later I would come to realize that my core superpower was actually strategy, and learning sales was strategic.

You have to start with whatever strength you have now, whatever you think you're the best in the world at. If it truly is a superpower, it will grow into something else. In the case of my son, his staring contest might just be a temporary strength—unless they create a sport and put it in the Olympics—but one day, he may come to realize that his superpower is actually an unwavering focus. Maybe when I'm fifty, I'll realize that I'm a great communicator, and not just a strategist. But for right now, it looks like I'm a strategist, and that's my greatest strength.

Ask your friends what they think your superpower is. What are you the best in the world at? Sometimes our strengths are more evident to other people than they are to us. (Or if you don't feel you can trust your friends' opinions, go to StrengthsFinder .com and take the test.) But don't ask people what they think your weaknesses are—if you have to ask others what your weaknesses are, be prepared for a long list, because if *you* don't see them, there are probably a hell of a lot of others who do.

CHAPTER 5
YOUR FAILURE QUOTIENT

When I was a kid, I worked the recycling center behind the grocery store, redeeming cans. My racket was pretty simple: I'd go out and collect cans at night, then the next morning, redeem them. At this job, I was exposed to some of the lowest forms of life I had ever seen. I'd arrive at 7 a.m. with the junkies, who would be dragging bags of aluminum cans into the receiving area behind the supermarket. They were looking for a couple of dollars for a fix, and I was trying to get some extra spending cash. The place smelled like piss, because that's what the addicts would fill the cans with, trying to tip the scales in their favor. My job was to empty their cans of urine, cigarette butts, and whatever else was in there, hand them in, get my redemption certificate, and go get some cash from the market. It was by far the dirtiest rock-bottom job I've ever had. And if I ever again have to do something just to make ends meet, it will not be that.

Next I worked at a dry cleaner. The shop was owned by some very small people, and the place was designed for them. Even as a teenager I was tall—six foot three—and I cannot tell you how many times I hit my head on one of the racks, or looked up, only to get sprayed in the face by steam or chemicals. That job lasted a day. I decided after my first shift, with a head full of lumps, that it wasn't for me.

I had some paper routes when I was a kid. I also got fired from some paper routes, too. There were a lot of hills in my neighborhood, and I refused to deliver a newspaper to a house that was a half a mile up a hill. It just didn't make sense. Every day the guy would call the newspaper office and complain that he didn't get a paper. And every day I would refuse to bike up that hill to deliver it. I was hoping that he would quit calling. Instead, my route manager waited at the end of my route to catch me just riding by that hill, and decided to let me go. Newspaper subscriber: 1, Me: 0.

Next, I took a job at a frozen-yogurt store. I was sixteen, and on the job I wore a bonnet over my hair and a nice white apron. One day Maureen McCormick, the actress who played Marcia Brady on *The Brady Bunch*, came in to get a yogurt. I was starstruck—I had grown up watching her on TV—so I made an effort to be extra polite while taking her order. I thought it was so cool that I got to meet a celebrity. In fact, I was trying so hard to charm her that I forgot to put the lid on the blender when I was making her yogurt smoothie. Needless to say, "Marcia Brady" wasn't charmed at all by the chocolate stains all over her white blouse and in her hair. At this point, my career serving frozen yogurt ended—I was fired.

These are my rock-bottom jobs. You might be in the worst job of your entire life right now. A total rock-bottom moment. Or worse, maybe you don't have a job at all. You might be thinking that from where you're at, being a rock-star anything is impossible. It's not. Life is all about finding out what you *don't* like doing, and then finding a way to not do it. And the process of selection and self-discovery never ends. I shared with you some of my worst, absolute rock-bottom jobs to make the point that if I had given up hope at any of these points, I would not be the man I am today. And you shouldn't give up hope either.

Take the Stairs

Success rarely comes without setbacks, but the irony is that failure is probably the least talked-about aspect of business. Mark Zuckerberg had very fast success, but we don't talk much about the crappy coding projects he was working on at Harvard before he put in enough time behind a keyboard to start Facebook, or the many missteps he's made since they made a movie of his life. Thomas Edison isn't known for the ten thousand ways he failed to figure out how a light bulb would work; he's known for inventing the light bulb.

As I've grown as a businessman, I've learned how to better

accept missing the mark than I did early on. I've failed time and time again. Because of my upbringing, I have built up a pretty high tolerance for friction over the course of my career, and I also have a positive belief about failure. To me, it's part of the process of success.

My first company, 24x7 Tech, didn't work out well on paper, and I lost money on it. When I sold my shares to my partner and left the company, I damaged my ego in the process; but in retrospect, it wasn't entirely a bad thing because it led me to create SkyPipeline. SkyPipeline wasn't that big of a hit either, because I went broke after selling it. But if I hadn't started SkyPipeline, I wouldn't have met the Goergens (the famous entrepreneurial family you will hear more about as you read this book) and learned how to be a CEO—and that was what I needed to start ViSalus. But at one point even ViSalus could have been considered a failure. When we sold to Blyth in 2008 and then almost went out of business during the recession, or when we nearly ran out of money in 2010, or when the company dropped from $600 million down to $200 million—these were all humbling experiences that some labeled as failures. I did not.

You can look at it two ways. You can see your career as a roller coaster of peaks and valleys, or you can see it as a set of stairs going upward. I'd rather take the stairs. 24x7 Tech might not have been a moneymaker for me, but I still learned how to build a million-dollar company. SkyPipeline became a $25 million company, and ViSalus was sold at a price of $792.4 million—so the mistakes I made were actually steps I took that allowed me to climb at a steady rate of growth over a twenty-year career.

The point is, what looks like a complete disaster today can look very much like a success ten or fifteen years from now; it all depends on your philosophy and your willingness to take a long-term perspective.

In *Nothing to Lose*, I talk a lot about figuring out your tolerance for risk. A risk quotient is when you ask yourself how much risk you can take starting a business venture; with a failure quotient, on the other hand, the risk has already happened, and you're asking yourself how ready you are—and how capable you feel—about embarrassing yourself or letting other people down. A failure quotient is a very real thing. When you fail, it's harder for you to do the next thing. They say you're only as good as the last thing you did, and if that "last thing" was a bad investment, or losing your home, or ruining your credit, people will judge you on that. Believe me, I know.

You have to get familiar with taking risks and sometimes failing. Embrace them, and figure them into the equation. What is your tolerance for failure? If you place a bet fifty times and it fails every time, will you still place the bet the fifty-first time? And bet it all? Every entrepreneur has to understand their failure quotient—the ability to fail and bounce back from it.

Recently, my friend Don Yaeger asked me to join his Circle of Champions men's retreat for a tour of United States Military Academy West Point. One of the things that stuck with me about their culture of excellence was that at West Point they force each cadet to fail often, because failure gives them an opportunity to discuss their weaknesses and strengths. For instance, they make them play several sports, not just the ones they are naturally gifted at, and put them in situations where they will fail again and again. Colonel Bernard Banks, who hosted us that day and showed us around the campus, told us that they compared this process of failing to tearing a muscle a little bit every time you work out, in order to build it up. I came back from my trip with a sharper perspective on failure. You should anticipate failure, knowing that it will make you stronger and more well rounded.

In fact, if you haven't failed yet, I'd argue that you're doing something wrong. I've watched more than a few people who didn't fail enough times before they launched a hit product, tank because they couldn't handle their success, and they didn't calculate their failure quotient.

Here's a great example: In 2009, ViSalus created the Body by Vi Challenge, which would eventually break us out of the recession. To our amazement, it was a huge hit, bigger than anyone imagined. But we played that hand too long. We should have had a new campaign ready to go in 2014 when the momentum of the challenge inevitably peaked, and we didn't, because we hadn't failed enough to prepare ourselves for that level of success. Now we have a new playbook, one that figures in the failures that could occur as a result of having massive success with a single product or campaign.

I believe you have to be humbled a lot in life to create lasting success, and I'm not embarrassed to write about my failures because by the time you read this, they will likely be on the road to success, or in the business graveyard. No matter who you are, there will be setbacks in your career. These are an entrepreneur's battle scars—the marks to show the places where the world has knocked you down and you got back up again. Be fucking proud of them.

Seeing Neon

Before I bought the Neon Energy Drink company, the creator, Dakota Rea, came to me and told me he felt like he had failed. He had raised $1.2 million at age twenty-five, developed a product (that I loved), hired people, recruited distributors, and watched Neon become a million-dollar company—and yet all he could see were the negatives. He told me he had made some bad decisions regarding his infrastructure, and with his various stockholders. He had to sell the company, because at the rate things were going, he was losing customers and would have to fire all of his employees. His investors had started fighting and playing games with him, and he was going through hell. He was looking for a bailout.

After I had analyzed the situation, I told him he was wrong. He was a success. I said, "You did what myself, Nick, and Blake— all three of us multitalented, and with a lot of background experience and the backing of the Goergens—were able to do over the course of many years, in a very short time." It was like a light bulb went off in his head—he was already successful; he just didn't realize it. I ended up buying Neon in 2015, and gave him a lucrative deal, because I saw the positive in the negative. We took Neon from near zero in sales to five million its first year, expanded into fifteen countries, and now it's a company worth many millions, and soon to be hundreds of millions.

If you're an entrepreneur, it's guaranteed shit will go wrong. It's inevitable. Good employees will leave you. Your investors will turn on you. You might buy a house in foreclosure just to find out it's not worth as much as you thought it was. The dot-com industry, or whatever industry you are in, might go bust. The economy might spiral into another recession or worse yet, depression. But something *will* happen; that's business. It's difficult to assess your own progress objectively, especially when you are dealing with any of the above scenarios. If your business is still standing, chances are you've done a lot more than you've given yourself credit for. I suggest you have people in your life who have the wisdom to find the positives in the negatives, and who see you for your potential, have your back, and most important, they're there to help you achieve your goals.

Desires Are More Important Than Goals

I used to be obsessed with goal setting. I wrote out all my goals every year in a very disciplined fashion. I used to fill up notebooks with goals and if I was at a restaurant and didn't have a notebook on me I'd ask the waiter for a pen and I'd write them down on my napkin. As a leader, giving people concrete goals has long been an essential part of the way I've had success. I'm sure that somewhere along the way, you were also told that you should, as a general rule, set goals for yourself every year. Articulating clearly what you set out to do in life is a good practice; but I've learned that ultimately, the only thing that will decide which items on that list are actually going to come to pass, is how much desire you have for a particular achievement.

Our goals aren't always the same as our desires. Goals are like ambitions, and sometimes your ambitions change. Desire is a strong feeling of wanting something, and desires don't change, they grow. Goals are things we want to do; desires are things we *have* to do.

For example, I wanted to be a best-selling author. Nothing was going to get in the way of that. I took a manuscript I had been kicking around for years and found a literary agent to represent me. Then the literary agent got us a publisher. Two years later I had a best-selling title on the shelves. While I was writing the book, I experienced a number of life-changing and traumatic events—I became a single dad, my stepfather died, my mother went into a coma, my son was diagnosed with autism—and I could have put that pen down a hundred times and canceled the project, but I didn't. I was obsessed with writing the book, and because I was engaged in something I truly wanted, I had an unlimited amount of fuel. I didn't become a best-selling author by writing my goal on a sheet of paper with a bullet point next to it—I achieved it because I desired it.

Our desires never go away, they only get buried when we don't recognize and act on them. The only time I've felt regret is when I desired something and didn't pursue it. I've never lost a single night of sleep regretting not playing football in college, because I didn't really desire it in the first place. But if I had played football, I wouldn't have started my first business while I was in college, and that I would most definitely regret.

My point is that when you obsess over and desire something, and you believe that it's your purpose to do it, you will accomplish it. In retrospect, having failed so many times at so many different things, I often ask myself, what's kept me in the game this long? The answer is desire.

CHAPTER 6
IDENTIFY YOURSELF

When I was first approached by Nick Sarnicola and Blake Mallen to start ViSalus in November 2004, they had done most of the work related to starting the business— coming up with the name of the company, the Web site and domain, sales and training materials—and they had also found the most important piece: someone who had created a great product. When I went to the Henry Ford Health System in Detroit, Michigan, to meet Dr. Michael Seidman and shake his hand for the first time, I quickly understood that this was a man who had spent thousands of hours, over twenty years of his life, researching herbs and tinkering with nutrients in his beaker-filled lab to come up with an amazing supplement program. That afternoon, Dr. Seidman showed me around his lab and passionately told me about every test, experiment, peer-reviewed article, and finding related to his creations. Everything I ever saw in a science class was in that multimillion-dollar facility, including a mice maze where the effectiveness of different nutrients could be tested in real time. It reminded me of the movie *Weird Science*, which had left a big impression on me when I was a kid, and here I was headed deep into "weird science."

I wasn't raised in an environment that would have ever encouraged me to get into medical school, but I had been deeply involved in various computer sciences at this point, so I made an association between the two. At SkyPipeline, the broadband wireless service company I created, we sent zeroes and ones through the air to an antenna. In my understanding, Dr. Seidman was doing the same thing, except his zeroes and ones were nutrients that he was sending into the human body, and the cells were the receiver.

We are often told this myth that being a doctor or a lawyer are the best jobs on the planet, but that's not true. I'm not saying that I am better or smarter than a doctor, but that there is another option. I thought to myself, *What's better than being a doctor? Being the guy who employs doctors.*

I saw ViSalus as a potential home run because of Dr. Seidman—here was this genius inventor in a white lab coat, who had a terrific product, certified research, and patents, but didn't understand the elements of running a business. On the other side of things, I saw two relatively new entrepreneurs—Nick and Blake—who were fantastic at sales and marketing. I thought to myself that with Seidman's product knowledge, Nick and Blake's knowledge of selling, and my understanding of how to finance and scale a business—it was a perfect combination. That's why ViSalus worked out so well for all of us.

When I first started raising money for ViSalus prior to the Goergens buying it, they introduced me to one of the funds they'd put money into, GRP (now Upfront Ventures), where I met a venture capitalist by the name of Brian McLoughlin. Although Brian didn't invest in ViSalus, I maintained a relationship with him, and have been able to bounce ideas off him from time to time. One time Brian and I were having lunch in Century City, California, near his office, and he asked what I'd do after selling to Blyth, and I shared with him my idea for a venture capital fund of my own, HashtagOne. Brian went on to give me this priceless piece of wisdom; he said, "There are great businesspeople, and great product people, but rarely are they both."

I am a businessperson who has built a large portion of my wealth by identifying great product people. A great product person is a perfectionist who understands their product down to every last detail. They have taken complete responsibility for the product's creation. By the end of a meeting with any rock star product creator, like Dr. Seidman for instance, I've likely seen every plan, reviewed all research, and heard every adjective that exists to describe their product. It gets to the point where I can't talk with them about the product anymore. They are maniacal about the details, especially the failures or imperfections of competing products. The founder of Neon Energy Drink is an excellent example. By the time we finished our talks about the drink, I was like, "Dakota, I'll buy the company, but for the love of God, if I hear you tell me how Red Bull and Rockstar are infe-rior one more time . . ."

As an investor and executive, I don't want to be the product expert in the boardroom—that's someone else's job—but I do want to be inspired by them and work with them. When I'm looking for seed-stage companies to invest in, I'm looking for great product people because I bring a lot of the business expe-rience. I'm just as obsessed with investing, growing, scaling, and selling companies as product people are obsessed with making great products. For example, Sirkus, a company I recently in-vested in, is run by a solid product team that needed help with financing and scaling the business. That's why I joined their board and invested.

A lot of entrepreneurs I meet don't have all the components to create a great company. For example, many are terrible at raising money; that doesn't bother me because that's where I can add value. In fact, as a seed-capital investor, it's a red flag to me when an entrepreneur is *too* good at raising money. In all but a few cases, when I've encountered an entrepreneur who has been very successful at raising money, it usually means that they don't spend enough time on their business.

The key is to identify what you're strong at and surround yourself with people who can offset your weaknesses. For in-stance, Ethan Anderson is a CEO I recently invested in who founded a company called MyTime. Here is a former Google exec who built a great company, he's a solid product person, and he's surrounded himself with a fantastic team and great board of directors to help him scale his business. That's why our fund,

HashtagOne, invested. Another example, one of my longtime protégés Jade Charles founded a tech start-up, Fragmob, and went from being an introverted software engineer to learning how to be a CEO of a business that's worth nearly $10 million. It hasn't been easy for him, but his evolution has helped him create a successful business. And you guessed it—that's why we invested.

All told, we've sold nearly $2 billion in products at ViSalus, so I know a thing or two about great products. In my experience, great products come from iteration. ViSalus is in the consumer health products category and has to deal with complex formulations that require hundreds of ingredients; you have to constantly tweak them. If you follow me on social media, you'll see I'm always testing our products, literally sometimes trying ten different variations of a product just to get the taste right. A standard future-products meeting with our R&D scientists can last three or four hours. Can you imagine how I feel after I've eaten one hundred bowls of cereal in six different types of milk? It's crazy. But that's how fanatical we are about great products. And that's why our products have been served nearly a billion times.

In 2014, the cofounders of ViSalus and I approached John Maxwell for mentorship, a renowned leadership expert who's authored over seventy books on the subject. During these mentoring sessions, he'd go around the room and ask what was frustrating us. One of my biggest frustrations at the time was that whenever I sponsored new products, I would hand them off to the team, and by the time of the launch, it was either nowhere near our original vision, they'd missed the point entirely, or it wasn't done to my level of quality. There was no way I could be involved in the details of every product created for a company that was in fifteen countries. That's when John gave me a genius formula for project creation: 10 percent/80 percent/10 percent. If you're a product person, you should be 100 percent involved. But if you're more on the business side, you should be engaged for the first 10 percent of the product's development, and then you should reduce your engagement and let other people handle it for the 80 percent. Don't get me wrong, you can check in during the 80 percent, but you absolutely have to be there for every last task of the final 10 percent until the product is launched.

I once hired Ken Segall, the guy who wrote the book *Insanely Simple: The Obsession that Drives Apple's Success,* to speak to my team. He worked closely with Steve Jobs, and I consider myself a lifelong student of Jobs, so I wanted to learn from him. I asked him whether Jobs was a great product guy or a great business guy. He told me he'd watch Steve playing for hours on the iPhone, testing and experimenting. Steve was an obsessive product person, but he was also involved in nearly every detail of his company. When he was done with the product, he'd hand it off to someone he trusted while he focused on other things. Even someone like Steve Jobs, who had the rare combination of being great at both products and business, knew when it was time to pass the baton, knowing he would get it back for the launch (the last 10 percent).

Great product people are divas (if you find yourself questioning this, you're probably one of them). They are so busy working on product creation that they have no energy or time left for anything else—even to sell you their products. They sleep in the office, they forget to answer their phones, and you have to demand a meeting just to get an update. That's the product person you want, or want to be. And a great product is so well designed and documented that not one detail is missing, including a road map for every milestone, every new version, and for the life cycle of the product. That's right, every product has a life cycle. I've learned this the hard way—that sometimes your passion for your creation outlives its place on the shelf. As a result, we have a process at ViSalus during which we do product rationalization and kill off products that have outlived their life cycles—you don't want five thousand products, you want fifty great ones. As a businessperson that's how you need to think about products.

People who are great at business aren't that different from great product people. Both are passionate. Business people are always looking for the next idea, product, project, or company in which to invest their time or money. They obsess over companies, culture, industries, processes, and avidly study economic and business cycles. They want to know the formula that makes a business successful, as much as a product person seeks to design a more energy-efficient light bulb or invent a new piece of technology. If you combine these two types of business people together you're almost guaranteed success.

So, what kind of businessperson are you? Are you a product genius? Are you a rock star at business? Does your company sell products or services or a combination of both? Are you a platform? A call center? Figure out your identity now and own it, otherwise you'll end up saying yes to the wrong things and no to the right ones. And never forget my favorite mantra: Focus is saying no.

Elevator Pitch

One night I was up writing an e-mail to Dan Gilbert, the owner of Quicken Loans. I wanted to ask his advice about moving our corporate headquarters from Troy, Michigan, to one of his buildings in downtown Detroit, and get his mentorship on the issue.

Dan is an icon and a multibillionaire, and I've been blessed to spend time with him. I wanted to be clear in my communication in this e-mail, but it was midnight, and I was fighting to stay awake. I started typing, explaining to him the condition of ViSalus and what we were up to, trying to keep it brief. As I was putting the final touches on it, I accidentally hit "Send." I thought: *Fuck. What did I write?*

I dug into my sent mail folder and reread the e-mail. (I'm a bad speller, so I knew there were going to be typos in there.) It turned out that in my unedited and misfired e-mail I had written a statement that very clearly communicated what ViSalus was. The statement was this: We make great products that get people results, then we market those results, and teach our distribution channel how to do the same.

That's it. That's all we do as a company.

Somehow it took eleven years to come up with a solid elevator pitch for my company. The irony is, I've even been a featured guest on MSNBC on a segment of a show where people pitched me their ideas in an elevator and I would judge their responses—and it took me over a decade to come up with one I'm proud to call my own.

If you're trying to write your own elevator pitch, my suggestion is to do what I did, and write an e-mail to somebody you admire so much you wouldn't want them to dismiss you. You don't have to send it, but start a draft and address it to Warren Buffett, Bill Gates, Mark Zuckerberg, Elon Musk, or someone else you respect and would do anything to have involved in your career. What would you say to this person, knowing that they're busy and probably have no time whatsoever? If you are only allowed a few words to say, and still leave a lasting impact on the person you're writing to, what would you write?

I stumbled on this technique by accident and it works for me, but you may not love writing late-night elevator pitches to entrepreneurs you've never met before. So, test it out on your friends. Or your family. Or go to a pitch night or a business plan competition at a local university.

It's not an easy thing to do. As a creative person, you see so much opportunity, novelty, beauty, and uniqueness in what you do that it's almost impossible to boil it down to a few short sentences. But once you do, you are all but unstoppable.

In early 2015, ViSalus was raising $15 million for growth capital and my partner Nick suggested we have a meeting with Tony Robbins, a personal mentor of his. I've been a big fan of Tony's for quite some time, but I had never met him, so I jumped at the opportunity. He had limited time that day and he offered to meet us on the runway at the Palm Beach International Airport in Florida, where his jet was getting ready to take off. I'll never forget driving to the tarmac and seeing his Boeing Global Express, a seventy-five-million-dollar plane, with the insignia T.R.

on the tail. (I knew Tony was big, but had no idea he was Global-Express big.) We boarded the plane and sat down on monogrammed leather seats, next to a bouquet of beautifully cut, hand-picked roses, and a tray of cookies and assorted desserts. There I was sitting knee-to-knee with Tony and Nick on my right. Immediately Tony and Nick started to make small talk about family and other things, and then Tony turned his attention to me suddenly and said, "Why are you raising money?"

My response was, "To invest in operations, new products, and to consolidate some of our multiple offices into one single location."

Tony immediately asked, "What decisions would you make differently if you had the money?"

I said, "I'd move quicker than I am now."

Tony appeared to be satisfied with my answers, and he turned back to Nick and said, "You have a child on the way, don't you?"

With a guy like Tony you only get one shot. There I was pretending to listen to them talk about their families, but really I was replaying the "tape" of what I said in my head saying, *Fuck, did I miss my opportunity?*

After a few seconds, abruptly, Tony turned back to me and asked, "What do you love about your company?"

I wasn't prepared for that question, but my first instinct was to say, "The people."

Clearly I was being tested. There are things that you love about your company and there are things that you hate, and entrepreneurs are problem solvers, so we tend to spend most of our time obsessing over what's not working than on what is. So, it's really easy not to have a spontaneous answer to that question. That's the nature of entrepreneurship.

"What do you love about the people?" Tony asked.

"Helping them," I said.

"What do you help them do?" Tony asked.

The questions were coming in rapid fire and I felt I was digging myself into a hole. I broke the flow of the interrogation by telling him a story about how when I was seventeen years old a mentor came into my life and taught me entrepreneurship and a better way of living life, and that now I help others just as I was helped. And that's why I love my company.

Basically, besides trying to figure out whether I was the real deal or not, Tony was asking me to identify myself—who I am and what type of person I am—because there are all types of businesspeople out there. I had less than ten minutes on that plane to deliver my proverbial "elevator pitch" to him, and I had to be satisfied with my answers. I may never work with Tony in any capacity, but thanks to his questioning I now realize that what I love most about my company is the people, and if I am ever asked again to identify myself in the context of my business I can say: I am the type of entrepreneur who loves to work with other great entrepreneurs. They say who you are is what you love. So, that's who I am.

Now it's time to identify yourself. What do you love about your business, and why?

CHAPTER 7

BEFORE YOU LAUNCH

was in a restaurant with my friend Wilmer Valderrama, the actor, and we were geeking out about business. I decided to demo for him a new app that tracks my company's sales in real time, one of the first of its kind. I proudly pulled out my cell phone and hit "Refresh," and to my surprise the sales jumped $1,000. I refreshed it again, and sales went up another $1,000. And then another $1,000. And another. I was speechless.

Wilmer smiled and said, "Dude! That is so nice!"

During the course of the meeting, he watched ViSalus make an extra $100,000. Soon after, we were doing $87,000 an hour in sales, twenty-four hours a day, seven days a week: $65 million a month.

Momentum is fucking amazing. Once a product (or a service) gets momentum, all of a sudden, in your sleep, you're making money. It is the holy grail of entrepreneurship. It all comes down to how you launch—the initial momentum—and when it comes to launching products, you only get one shot. (Cue Eminem's "Lose Yourself.")

Today's consumers are in an extremely noisy marketplace. We are exposed to thousands of ads every day—from our Starbucks coffee logo to the apps on our phones to the label on the brand of whiskey we drink at happy hour. We can't sit there and fully process every targeted ad we come across, so we cope with the excess by deleting information. *Delete. Delete. Delete.* Launching a product is about breaking the sound barrier, so to speak. The same way a jet has to get enough velocity to do it, so does your message. You have to break through the noise of all the other people who are trying to market their products to your prospective customers, so that they stop deleting information just long enough to receive your message. And if you're good, they won't delete you, too.

I haven't always been good at launching products. I've gotten it wrong so many times, mostly with tech products. With software, you tend to get excited about all the bits and bytes that make up the product. But today's user doesn't care about five hundred features. Nobody has time to review all the features of a product—they are looking for the least amount of information needed to confirm their desire to make the purchase. Think about the last time you used all the features of a product. Features are easy to rip off. The best products are cleverly designed so that you discover more features as you go. This is a very hard thing to grasp, especially for people like me who want to create something truly great; we have a tendency to want our products to do everything.

When Steve Jobs introduced Apple's first iPhone, he rolled it out as a Web browser, a music player … and a phone. The phone was the last part. He didn't say to the world, "Here's a better phone." He simplified and reverse-engineered his launch to appeal to consumers in the short amount of time he'd have their attention. Another company would have rolled it out as a phone with a focus on its seventy-five features, and that would have been that—creating more noise instead of breaking the sound barrier.

Every six months at ViSalus we launch new products. We are religious about our product launches. What I mean is that we don't question the process; there's a certain time and place, and we spare no time, effort, or energy for our launch. I've launched hundreds of products in my career, and I've gotten them into fifteen countries. We recently launched a Vi-Shape® Superfood Shake. I could go on and on about the twenty-five vitamins and minerals, the fact that it's vegan and has very few grams of sugar—but I know that you're going to find out all that after you buy it. And the only way you'll buy it is if first I've communicated why you should buy it before I tell you what's in it.

When I launched *Nothing to Lose*, I was an unknown author, releasing my first book during August, traditionally a low season. I knew that if I did this, it might gain momentum. I put so much into my launch: creating entrepreneurial webinars for readers, sending galley copies to my network, staging giveaways and running competitions, booking myself solid with speaking engagements, book signings, and appearances—I knew I had to break that sound barrier. The hardback edition hit number three on the *New York Times* best-seller list in the August sales lull, became the number one business book and number one paperback in 2013, and went on to become an international best seller. Five years later it is still prominently on the shelves. The secret was in the launch. I put everything I could into the product, and then I turned my sights to the launch. I broke through the noise, and from there the product began to sell on its own.

I've had a few projects hit what Malcolm Gladwell called the "tipping point"—the point at which a series of small events becomes significant enough to spark a larger, more important change. The funny thing about tipping points is that the guy in the middle of one is the only person who knows he's experiencing a tipping point. If you ask the experts or the critics, they're going to say, "It'll never last!" Right after the launch of the book, in late 2011, I went to *Inc.* magazine to do a one-hour video session with them, where readers asked me questions. One asshole got on and started saying that "according to the Blyth SEC filings" I was a fraud, and all my success was actually fake. He spent the entire time tearing me apart, according to one data point: the prior years' sales at ViSalus. What he didn't know was that I was soon on my way to creating a billion dollars in sales, and millions of people would be buying and/or consuming my content and products. He didn't know the thousands of seemingly minor chess moves that had been accumulating over the years to create my tipping point. He knew the entrepreneurial "tale of the tape," but he didn't know that I had perfected the launch. He also didn't know that the very act of his commenting was actually part of the strategy and that he was unwittingly helping me launch.

Launches aren't easy. By the time you're ready to launch that new piece of software, your groundbreaking documentary, or the next great American novel, you're tired. You put everything you had into the product, and maybe you're broke—but you're hopeful. You've had your head in the creation process, in the planning and the details. You have to shift your thinking from product developer to entrepreneur, and rally the energy around launching the product flawlessly so you can gain traction and make back your investment.

In my experience, the launch is the hardest part. Get it right and your product is immortalized, get it wrong and you're gone. Launching a product is a developed skill that requires the right process, and the process I use, and the one we use at ViSalus, is a two-part launch. You dive into your contacts list and sort it into two categories: the mavens/influencers (to borrow another term from Gladwell) and the immediate customers. First, a soft launch; you focus on the customers, all the people who will buy your product or service right away (yes, your mother counts), and immediately sell the product to them. Then, you approach the mavens, product experts, and those with the most influence in your network. You've got some sales under your belt now, and you can confidently offer them a discount or a free trial, or ask them to beta test with you and your product-launch team— mavens love being part of a new innovation. Google is the master at this, as well as Microsoft. Gmail was in beta for five years . . . if it isn't still.

When you communicate with the influencers, you're talking about features and benefits. It's the only time you have permission to go deep into the many features of your product that make it great. To use my ViSalus products as an example, my influencers are technical experts, dieticians, nutritionists, health and wellness professionals, and doctors. It's important to communicate the nitty-gritty details of the features to them specifically (and only them).

We're all looking for that coveted tipping point, so here is an action plan to refer to for your next launch:

1. Build your prospect list and sort it. Who is most likely to buy now? Get those sales and that early momentum.
2. Soft launch. Identify those on your list who have influence. These mavens take the most work to win over. Call them and say, "I have a hundred people who just bought this. Take a look."
3. Attempt the cold market. Take out an ad, post shareable content, and drive leads.
4. Optimize. Look at the data—were the consumers a different demographic than you'd expected? Does the price need to be adjusted?
5. Make adjustments and market them.
6. Target your best customers.
7. Rinse and repeat.

(Note that by reading this book, you bought it during one of these seven steps.)

In my opinion, the difference between being a "thousand-aire" and a millionaire is the desire to do the work, leave no stone unturned, and deal with the rejection and criticism that is inevitable with any launch. You have to believe so much in whatever the hell you're doing that nobody can tell you otherwise. Anytime I've failed to launch, I didn't have the belief, or I thought I could leverage prior success, and I didn't put my all into the liftoff.

The good news is that you can always relaunch a product. It isn't easy to do, but if you have to relaunch something, and you tell a new story, it is possible to succeed. But, trust me, it's much easier to plant the seed of a story than it is to change it. So many companies set their reputations in stone and become typecast, the same way actors find themselves unable to break out of their most popular roles. Consumers' perceptions, once solidified, are difficult to break—it takes ten times the amount of work than when you first put the story in their heads. I've used my company's entry into weight loss as an example later on in this book; once the mass majority of the consumer market saw ViSalus as one of the top five diets in the world, that perception was permanent. Keep this in mind.

Now, when we look at acquiring a product or a company, we always ask ourselves, "What is the promise we're going to make to the individual using this? Can we honor it? Is it worth it?" Because once we've invested in it, from there we have to launch it. We get one shot to break the sound barrier. And we won't hold anything back.

The Certainty Formula

I tend to think of things in mathematical terms, and so I created a little mathematical test for product launches: the certainty formula. It gave me a tool I could use to rally my team around new designs before they went into production. Because if your entire team isn't certain you have the right plan, the product is predestined for failure.

I approach my team with a new product that I'm absolutely positive is going to be great. I get feedback and ask each person to quantify their confidence in the product. How certain are you, on a scale of one to ten, that this design is going to be great? In the event that the average score in the room is lower than mine, I know that I have to double down on building up their confidence. Confidence comes from belief, and beliefs are created through communication. So that's what I do when I sense a lack of certainty—I communicate.

One of the biggest challenges of launching a new product is when you're certain it will succeed, but everyone else isn't. You need the certainty of your team behind you, so don't make the mistake of getting lazy—do the work and spend the time and energy making sure that your certainty formula works out before moving forward. Then you can fire on all cylinders to take off.

Out-Innovate the Competition

One of the reasons I started focusing on the direct-selling industry, despite my prior distaste for it, was that I saw an extreme lack of innovation among its companies. I'm hyper-competitive, and I like my companies to drive innovation in an industry, so it seemed like a good challenge for me. I chose a start-up that had focused its energy on being an innovative disrupter.

But there is a downside; the irony of being the innovation leader in an industry is your competition will simply copy you. I thought that if we all focused on innovation, the game would be "may the best innovator win." That's not the case—sometimes it's the best *copier* who wins. (We're using Facebook, not Myspace, right?) I received a report the other day that listed sixty-three companies in my industry that have copied some element of ViSalus's business model. Just thinking of it makes the hair on the back of my neck stand up. (I've literally heard my exact phrases come out of other CEOs' mouths.) This used to drive me crazy, but now I see it as a sign that it's time to get back to innovating.

A lot of companies along the way have given me competitive anxiety, but generally, if you have good business values, a good strategy, great people, and these people also have a working structure—you shouldn't worry about your competition. The company with the best products that provide the best value will have the best chance of survival, while companies that are simply cloning others will fall by the wayside in time. In the end, consumers have a choice, and that wins out. So, pace yourself, because a few years from now, you won't be dealing with the same tasteless imitators. (I can name more than two hands' worth of our competitors that no longer exist over the twelve years I've spent at ViSalus.)

There are brilliant people out there; the best way to innovate is to find them and hire them. I have learned to do this the hard way. I'd rather spend a dollar on hiring the right people from my competitors than a dollar on an attorney to fight a competitor. They can't copy culture, passion for the end user, and intelligence. So, let them steal your quotes, and try to take credit for your ideas, while you spend your energy getting ahead in other ways. As Napoleon said, "Never interfere with your enemy when he is making a mistake."

CHAPTER 8
FUNDING FIRST

You've probably heard this before: It takes money to make money. First off, it isn't true, unless maybe you're playing the stock market. And second, it's discouraging, because it makes people think that in order to be financially successful they need to have already accumulated wealth. I don't know who came up with the expression, but money doesn't make money—*you* make money. And if you have money, you make it make money, too.

As you've probably figured out from reading this book, there were a lot of times during my career as an entrepreneur when I was broke or very nearly so. There are going to be points in your career when you're going to face not having enough money, going bankrupt, trying to raise money, or starting again from scratch. I have never let not having money stop me from moving toward my goals. There are so many paths to financial success, but subscribing to this mind-set about needing money to make money isn't going to get you there. If you don't have money, you have to raise it.

I recall one meeting I had with some entrepreneurs from a start-up I'm on the board of. They confided in me that they were running out of money, and by December they'd be broke (it was November). This is a company we've put nearly $7 million into, and I've brought them plenty of investors over the years. I was like, *What the fuck?* Besides the fact that they didn't bring this to my attention two months earlier, when they should have, it was ridiculous that I had to explain to them what it means to be the boss.

I looked at the CEO and said, "Your number one job is to make sure you have enough money in the bank at all times. If you can't do this through sales—the preferred method—then go raise money."

It reminded me of the time I overheard my good friend and fellow entrepreneur, Sam Ben-avraham, having some words with one of the members of his camp at Burning Man. The guy was apparently telling Sam how he couldn't help break down our camp because he had to go home. Sam just said, "There's your issues, and then there's my issues. That's *your* issue." Sam made it clear that if the guy didn't help clean up the campsite, he wouldn't be welcome back. I had never before heard something so simply put. And I can't count the amount of times after I heard this that I've deployed his exact words in business.

In my mind, it was this CEO's job to raise money. That was his issue, not mine. Your number one job as an entrepreneur is to make sure you have money in the bank. Secondarily, your job is to build, hire, sell, etc. Whether you're the CEO of a company, or you work for a corporation managing a large department, or you're inventing a new product with a small team—you have to get funded first.

We all have the same difficulties raising money; there's a lot of competition. However, these days there are many options, and if you can't find private investors, then you can crowdfund. A team at Marvel Comics recently raised a couple million dollars for a new character through crowdfunding, and now they have built-in marketing because the crowd feels a connection to the character. This team didn't steal from their existing budget, they didn't scrap the idea, and they didn't go begging for funds from upper management—they figured it out.

One of my best returns on investment was a company called Elite Daily. When I first met them, as millennial entrepreneurs, they had few resources, but they were resourceful. As entrepreneurs, they didn't sit there and say, "I can't make this amazing product because I don't have the money." A boss doesn't say to his most innovative employees, "Sorry, we don't have enough money to do that." A great boss, executive, or entrepreneur will always find a way to get the resources to make their best ideas come to life. Period.

In 2010, when we were fund-raising for Fragmob, I approached my business partner Todd Goergen and asked to borrow money. Of course, he said, "Why do you need it?"

I told him, "Hey, Captain Obvious—I need it because I need it."

Of course I was putting this cash directly into Fragmob, but he didn't need to know that. He needed to trust me.

Every month I would ask him for another loan, and he gave it to me, mostly without question. Finally, one day Todd said, "Ryan, I'm not a bank. When are you going to pay me back and when are you going to stop borrowing money from me?"

And that's when I showed him. I'll never forget the excitement in his voice when I told him what we had done with our new mobile software and his money—he was impressed. And then I broke the news to him: I said, "I'm not paying you back."

The look on his face indicated I didn't quite stick the landing. So, I explained to him, I was giving him 50 percent of my interest in the business that he loaned me the money to build, and didn't even know it.

He said, "You built something of real value here. Why are you handing me half?"

I said, "That's what's fair. You trusted me and I trust you."

Not only did I prove to Todd that I could be trusted to do the right thing, but it cemented our friendship. And today, Fragmob is worth nearly $10 million, because we got funded. I took the risk, and made a bet on my entrepreneurial instincts.

Even the "Iron Man" himself Elon Musk had to put funding first to the point where he nearly went bankrupt during the 2008 recession after putting all his money from the sale of PayPal ($180 million) into his other three ventures, SpaceX, Tesla, and Solar City. The truth about his financial situation came out, embarrassingly, during his divorce proceedings. He had to borrow money from his friends for his living expenses. That's how hard he "funded first."

So, there is no excuse why your company doesn't have any money—unless you have a bad company that nobody wants to invest in. In which case, start a new company.

Once you have the money, managing it on the granular level is a whole different challenge. So many times I've had people come to me who have the funding they need, but haven't done any of the critical thinking on how they're going to spend it. In my mind, it takes the same amount of work to create a proper budget as it does to create a proper business model. If an executive comes to me with a plan for a $1 million marketing spend, I'd expect the same out of them as I would a start-up CEO presenting me with a $1 million investment opportunity. If you're the CEO, you're investing your shareholders' capital, and if you're not the CEO, you're spending money that's not yours. Prove to me why you need to.

I know very well what happens when money isn't spent correctly: the employees don't prosper, the shareholders don't make a return, you're unable to invest in growth initiatives, and the company comes to a standstill. It's like the Will Rogers quote I included in *Nothing to Lose*: "If you're on the right track, and you just stand there, you'll get run over." So, unless you're happy juggling a few hundred customers until the day when some piece of technology renders your business obsolete overnight—funding first.

CHAPTER 9
BUILD AND REBUILD

I n 2009, we changed our entire ViSalus business model twice in the first six months. I wouldn't advise it, and I wouldn't want to go through it again. It was aggressive, it was too much too fast, and it was risky. Had Nick, Blake, and I not been willing to hit the reset button a couple of times, we probably wouldn't have survived the "Great Recession."

We had fallen behind our competitors, and in an effort to catch up, we created a modernized back-end system for our distributors called Vi-Net, and made significant changes to our compensation plan. We rolled out everything in February, just four months after we closed the deal with Blyth to sell the company.

Next, we brought in "big fish" sales leaders. These were top-earning sales pros from other companies in our industry. It was an ego decision on my part. I wanted to raid the same companies that had been raiding us, damaging our business over the past few years. We brought in too many outsiders at once, and we didn't have a good filter for who was aligned with our value system and who wasn't. We didn't have deep relationships with these people, and they weren't attached to us, nor were we to them. They had made their deals with the company, and nobody cares if they hurt a *company*. We were essentially writing checks to people we were hoping would work out, and I learned the hard way that hope isn't a strategy.

Our corporate strategy was flawed: when things aren't going well, if you get all the right people in all the right places, the problems will take care of themselves—or so we were thinking. Easier said than done.

All the work we put into these changes was only distracting us from our real problems, and the real solutions to them that we needed. Initially, we saw some improvement, some growth. But in May of 2009, it started falling apart. The company was losing $600,000 every month.

The deal we had made with Blyth, our parent company, when they bought ViSalus in 2008 was a drastic change, particularly for me. Having to answer to a publicly traded company and be accountable to the Blyth board made early 2009 unbelievably stressful. I had just had my son Reagan. The level of responsibility and accountability—and the expectation that we would operate as executives on a world-class level—was overwhelming at times. I would tell Nick and Blake, over and over, "You may think this is the greatest decision in the world, but I have to spend the next six hours of my life explaining to these people why we made it. And if it doesn't work, I then have to explain why it didn't work and what we're going to do about it."

We were used to doing things on our own without telling Blyth, or anybody else, about it first. The change we made in our compensation model was one of the first of many hard lessons. The changes we had made without notifying Blyth set it up so that when our business started to really deteriorate, they blamed it on the changes. In retrospect we needed to make the changes, but we went about it the wrong way in terms of communicating that to our partners at Blyth.

The company needed more funding, and it was my job to ask Blyth for it. The $5 million credit facility we had written into our agreement with Blyth made it possible for us to ask Blyth for more money, but they weren't just handing it over to us—it was a loan. Which meant that Nick, Blake, and I would have to repay it, out of our own pockets.

Of course, Nick, Blake, and I had spent the money we had gotten from the sale of ViSalus on new cars, new houses, taxes, and old debts. Now, more and more of that money in our newly acquired security blankets was going back into ViSalus (and mine into my newborn son), and the company was doing worse and worse.

Blyth beat the hell out of our team. How we presented information, how we thought about our financials, how we formulated strategy—none of it was good enough. Our youth, our inexperience, and the fact that we were still essentially in start-up mode—those were no longer valid excuses. We spent hours locked in meeting rooms, working on financial models and projections.

In the board meetings, Bob Goergen was relentless, and Bob's two sons, Todd and Rob, were molded after their father. Bob was a Wharton guy, in fact he endowed Wharton to create the Goergen School of Entrepreneurship, and clearly we would have never made it into that program. They threw concept after concept at us: strategic marketing plans, six sigma implementation, SKU rationalization programs—it was like going to Harvard Business School, except none of us had gone to Harvard Business School. I was the only one of the cofounders who had spent any time in business school, and either I wasn't paying attention during that time, or I left too early to get those lessons. I sat through most of those meetings feeling much like a ninth grader who looked at algebra for the first time and thought—*I'll never get this.*

It was a tough situation. Being the young executives that we were, with our pride on the line, we couldn't just say, "Hey, we have no fucking idea what any of this is."

Here Bob Goergen was, one of the four hundred richest Americans, five decades into his career, babysitting a bunch of unpolished executives who couldn't even comprehend what he's asking for. We had taken millions of dollars out of his pocket and put it into ours; his patience and his tolerance were wearing thin.

The tension between Bob and us, and our continual failure to meet his expectations of business acumen, started to deteriorate my friendship with Todd, and it put added pressure on my relationship with Nick and Blake, and even my employees. I had a newborn child to worry about, I stopped working out and gained weight, and the stress of feeling like I had failed was starting to take its toll on my health. During that time, I was at a meeting at Blyth and Todd's brother, Rob Goergen, had just given me a rash of shit in the boardroom—and I remember thinking, *I give up.* Afterwards, I pulled him aside, and said, "I may not be able to clearly articulate the strategy in your terms, but I have a plan."

Rob listened to me, but he didn't hear me. We were speaking two different languages.

The Challenge

I had met legendary Louisiana State University basketball coach Dale Brown in 2006, through my social networking start-up PathConnect. I invited him to be the keynote speaker at the ViSalus event where we would announce that Blyth had completed the purchase of ViSalus in October 2008. Onstage with me, he boasted that at seventy-three he was in better shape than I was. He looked straight at me sitting in the front row of the audience and said, "Ryan Blair, I challenge you to the Dale Brown challenge."

The Dale Brown challenge was this: Every day for 365 days, we would each run one mile and lift weights for one hour. If one of us didn't complete the challenge, we would have to call the other and say on national television, "I'm just a boy, calling a man."

He baited me perfectly and the crowd joined his enthusiasm. I was in.

Over the next few months the challenge became the only thing keeping me sane in a time of total chaos and uncertainty. In April, even as Reagan's mom was going into the early stages of labor, I was in the hospital room with her, lifting chairs and sprinting back and forth, counting each stride to hit a mile (there are 5,283 feet in a mile, in case you're wondering). Everyone thought I was crazy.

The challenge wasn't a distraction—instead, it kept me disciplined when business was all negativity. I would tell everyone about the challenge, and I discovered that people were interested in hearing my newest story about an odd workout. As soon as I mentioned it, they wanted to hear more. Friends of mine were either joining me, doubting me, or at least having a good laugh. Even the Blyth team would always ask, "How's that challenge going?" at the start of a meeting.

Friends, family, and associates—even my antagonists—were engaged by the idea of it. I saw the magic in that, and I was sure of one thing—whatever we created next, whatever we did to reinvent our struggling company, it had to have the word "challenge" in it.

Ever since coming aboard ViSalus as the CEO, I've been coming to terms with network marketing as an industry. I couldn't get past the idea that we were selling an entrepreneurial opportunity to people who may not have been entrepreneurs—who didn't have the drive, the salesmanship, the appetite for risk, or the ability to mitigate it. But the idea of selling a challenge was exciting to me. No company in our industry had done something like this before.

In his book *Onward: How Starbucks Fought for Its Life without Losing Its Soul*, Howard Schultz describes his passion for sitting down with a great cup of French roast coffee. Everything about Starbucks—how it grew, how it operates, decisions the company made through the tough times—rests on his love of coffee. Nick, Blake, and I didn't have that. We didn't know it at the time, but we needed this challenge, too.

This was the aftermath of the Great Recession. We were starting to see that we could lead with our Vi-Shake—an affordable meal replacement product—and it could become the point of focus. During recessions people want to save money and they are still interested in losing weight. And thanks to the U.S. economic downfall, they were now interested in saving money. The idea of a ninety-day health and fitness challenge was, in my opinion, a critical piece, but when I approached the team with it, I could feel their hesitation.

The Goergens listened to our ideas, but they had serious doubts. In a last-ditch effort, Blyth decided to hire a consultant to advise me. I willingly accepted the gesture as a good solution and as an opportunity to tune me up on my business skills. The consultant was a very likeable guy, with an animated personality. I opened the door, brought him into the office and into my home, and invited him to social events. I really tried to embrace him.

In one meeting, I laid out all my plans to him, and explained how we were trying to fix everything about the company and how the challenge would be our redemption. The consultant promised he'd help us put together our strategy and presentation. We worked for hours on it, in my home, and in different cities. I thought he was not only going to bring value and give us some good things to think about, but also report back to Blyth that we were working on the problem. Of course, he totally threw us under the bus.

Instead, he submitted a report to the board, basically telling them that we were a complete write off, and to fire me. I had to ask six different people, six different ways, to let me see that report. Finally, Todd reluctantly gave it to me. In bold letters the title read: "The Body by Vi Challenge Will Not Save ViSalus."

In retrospect, I should have noticed the difference between my frank, almost confrontational manner, and his fake exaggerated condescension. His two-faced demeanor hid the fact that he was internally identifying and targeting every one of our flaws. I later found out that he had been interviewing for my job. Not only was Blyth secretly sitting around discussing this report, but they were already trying to figure out how to replace me and with who.

I learned a valuable lesson about consultants—that when someone suggests a consultant to you, sometimes you should say no. The unscrupulous ones use their position as an outsider to gather intel, cherry pick the top positions, and plot ways to insert themselves inside them.

The recession had exposed challenges in our business that we weren't prepared to address. To our credit, we weren't the only executives with cracks in our foundation—Goldman Sachs, GE,

AIG, General Motors, Washington Mutual, and nearly all the businesses during this time had them too—but in the middle of the crisis, nobody was giving us much sympathy. We shouldn't have had the cracks in the first place, they said. And they were right. The consultant brought all those cracks front and center, and had not only humiliated me, but destroyed any remaining confidence Blyth had in us.

All I could do was keep hammering them with the solution right in front of us: The Body by Vi Challenge. I kept reiterating: It wasn't my idea. It was a Hall of Fame coach's idea, and it would create the level of engagement we needed. I would literally scream at people during meetings, "We are doing this!"

It was our last chance.

The Comeback

By the end of 2012, ViSalus was profitable; we made $97 million in profit that year. The Body by Vi Challenge had far exceeded our expectations.

The challenge was social. Now our sales force (we call them promoters) were no longer shoving an entrepreneurial opportunity down their friends' throats; instead, they were inviting them to join a challenge. Social support is a major part of success. I could finally connect emotionally, logically, and culturally to what we were doing as a company. We started with promoters we could get behind 100 percent, but now we had a model *I* could get behind 100 percent (I was still as much a customer as I was a businessman).

We constantly set challenges for ourselves. Blake competed in a national jiu-jitsu tournament and climbed Mt. Whitney. I used the challenge to complete a ninety-day Muay Thai challenge. We believed in the strategy, and we could see it in ourselves, our employees saw it, and our customers loved it. Three million people signed up for our challenge and we've sold nearly $2 billion in products since launching it.

We had found the key to getting people to use our products, talk about their results, and engage others in their success stories. We watched our consumers transform, and our company transformed with them. That was how the Body by Vi Challenge brought ViSalus out of its worst rock-bottom moment and launched it into stardom.

Your business model is a living thing—it connects to customers, social networks, communications systems—and if you're in a business like mine, it connects to people, and people change. The way you approach a customer today works today, but it might not work tomorrow. Everyone in business is either targeting your customer or supporting someone who is. All the businesses we have on this planet end with you, the consumer.

Today, your business model needs to evolve at a more rapid pace than ever seen before. And the only way to do that is to iterate an experiment until you find success, meaning that your customers are happy and you're selling your products or services at a profit. Then the moment that happens, you need to disavow yourself from your newfound sense of happiness and ask yourself—how can I tear this company apart? If I was my own competition, how would I take this customer from me? And with that lens you need to rebuild your business all over again.

The good news is that each time you rebuild it, you've added to your foundation more tools and resources, and more data, hard fought experience, and in some cases better instincts and a deeper understanding of your customers. But if you don't rebuild your business, someone else will build one to take you out of business.

The Reinvention Rule

Recently, I sat down with one of my mentors, John Maxwell, and at the end of the meeting, I asked him why he was spending time with me, when clearly he could be hanging out with presidents, or his friends, the CEOs of Fortune 500 companies. My question was, "What can I do for you?" Here's a man who started out as a pastor, then reinvented himself as a leader of pastors and taught others, then went from leader to author, and from author to business leader—and now he's considered the foremost business leader by a variety of authorities on the planet.

John smiled and said, "Legacy."

"Please explain," I said.

"I believe you'll make a large impact with the knowledge I hand down to you," John said.

John told me that his next reinvention is his legacy. To leave a lasting impact on the world.

Reinvention is the rule. All rock stars reinvent themselves, and the most successful at reinvention are the ones with the longest trajectories. Look at Madonna, who is in her fourth decade as an entertainer (at the time of this writing) and still a rock star. Many artists get their fifteen minutes of fame, but she's had so much more than that because she's perfected the art of reinvention. And this has given her longevity in a field that's generally dominated by youth in our culture.

Today, fifteen minutes of fame only pays ten minutes' worth of bills. This was one of my fears when I was writing my first book. How long would it be on the shelf? I went from tech entrepreneur to wellness entrepreneur to author, and from author to best-selling author. I was ecstatic when *Nothing to Lose* got translated into twelve languages, but I can't say I'm a global number one best-selling author yet. To have any chance of making that type of impact and leaving a lasting legacy, it will depend on what actions my readers take—whether or not you are inspired to share this message—and, when that fifteen minutes is up, whether I am able to reinvent myself once again in order to remain worthy of your attention.

CHAPTER 10
THE RIGHT SOLUTIONS

A common mistake I see companies make is trying to solve problems by hiring more people. I have studied problems, I have come up with strategies for fixing problems, and I have fired my way out of problems—but rarely have I hired my way out of one.

We all want to make money doing whatever it is that we do—but hiring people to come up with the answers isn't going to work for you. I'll give you an example. ViSalus was originally intended to be a health and wellness company focused on science-based supplements first and, secondarily, on weight loss. We launched a highly successful weight-loss product and a shake, and the next thing we knew, we were a weight-loss company. The problem was, we didn't know a lot about weight loss. Our mission wasn't weight loss. So my executives said, "We need to start hiring." We hired almost five hundred people to solve all the problems we couldn't solve ourselves. They failed miserably, and so did we.

We are still learning about weight loss at ViSalus; it's a highly competitive and rapidly evolving industry. But now that we've stopped trying to outsource our problems, and learned to solve them ourselves, when opportunities arise—like the holidays, when our consumers are thinking about weight loss—we are also thinking about weight loss.

Say you have a sales problem, your numbers are stagnant, and you desperately need sales. You decide to hire someone, or better yet ten people. You have a 50 percent chance that the people you've just hired won't work out—it's just that simple. You need revenue, and your sales problem just got bigger. Or say they do work out and they might be able to solve the problem, but it's going to take them twice as long as you expected because they are brand new. Your sales problem just got bigger. Or maybe if you decide to hire a consultant instead of an employee, they might be able to tell you how other companies have solved that same problem, but they cannot solve your problem. You'd better learn sales. Or marketing. Or product development. Or whatever it is that is going to help your company be the best at what it does. You can't outsource problems, but you can fix them by becoming the solution.

Take Note

If you think you need diligent people more than you need a solid business model, you're in for trouble.

I used to believe that seeing people taking notes during meetings was an indicator of their engagement. That's what we're told to do when we want to impress our bosses, teachers, or clients: take notes. This is actually a poor indicator of real engagement. I'm a note taker—you'll rarely see me without a journal—but the only time I take notes during a meeting is when I need a memory jogger (or when you're boring the hell out of me with a Power-Point presentation, and I'm writing down who I need to talk to to have you fired—or reminding myself to call my mom). If something is truly important, you'll commit it to memory, and you won't need a notebook. If you have a bad memory, there are supplements for that.

When someone is truly engaged, they're seeking clarity; they'll come back to you with thoughts and arguments. They'll disagree with you constructively. They'll make you repeat yourself, and they'll ask questions. Ideally, I want to see someone so committed to the conversation it's like they are speaking with the president of the United States. That's the level of engagement I want and try to bring. If they must scribble something down in their notebook while I'm talking, they'll excuse themselves to write it down by asking me to pause so they can take a note, commit it to memory, and take action. I'm okay with that. But once you get good at deciphering actionable items, you realize there's only a few times when you have your notebook out: to learn and to write down actions.

Poorly engaged individuals are easy to spot. They are the ones sitting in the conference room because they want to look like they are doing their jobs, not because they can add value to the conversation, or even want to. They just want enough information so they can go back to their bosses and make themselves look good—or look just good enough to make someone else look bad. Most of them don't give a shit about the products, the agenda, or the people in the company. I can't tell you how many times I've sat in board meetings with a variety of different companies and looked around the room at these disengaged people, thinking, *Why the hell are you here?*

I don't want to see a room full of people taking notes. I want eye contact with engaged individuals.

Similarly, who came up with the rule that all presentations had to be put into PowerPoint?

One of my favorite entrepreneurs, the founder of Amazon .com, Jeff Bezos, requires his executives to write four- to six-page memorandums called "narratives" on the subjects they'll be presenting. He doesn't allow PowerPoint presentations at all. His argument is that sitting down to craft a narrative structure in a four-page memo forces better thought processes and a deeper understanding of the importance of subjects, and how they interrelate. He compares a PowerPoint presentation to making a bulleted list in Word, allowing the presenter to gloss over ideas, and their connection to a subject. In other words, it's lazy.

If you have to sit down and write four pages, you have to

make tradeoffs, you have to do some homework, and you have to thoroughly understand what it is you are trying to express. In a further step, Bezos makes presenters sit in the boardroom and read the narratives aloud, going around the table, taking thirty minutes for each one, word by word. There's intelligence behind this, and it's high-level.

I cannot tell you how many times I've seen people get up in front of a packed room and stand there selling a PowerPoint presentation full of bullet lists and bullshit. It's too easy. I've hired experts who I've sometimes paid millions of dollars to throw a bunch of loosely related ideas into PowerPoint and call it a presentation. It makes me wonder—do they even really know what they are talking about? Or are they just coasting through life until the day comes when they can call a vendor to fix their problems—and stick me with the bill?

Don't get me wrong, PowerPoint is great for getting through numbers and one-page presentations, but it's not for selling your big ideas, or a replacement for writing a proper executive summary. I'm with Bezos on this one.

The Company Is You

I learned early on that it wasn't hard work that made money, it was working hard at the right things. But the more people you're responsible for, the more that mentality creeps back in. You think you owe it to them to work the longest hours, even if you're not putting your effort into the right projects. You can forget that your people need the right solutions from you, not the most solutions.

Back in the SkyPipeline days, I would always feel pissed off at myself if I wasn't the first person to show up at work in the morning. Even if I was fifteen minutes late, I would feel guilty as hell. I used to believe that as the CEO, I needed to show up at the office at exactly 6 a.m., every Monday, and be the last one to leave.

Now I work from home on Mondays. If I decide I don't want to show up on Monday, I don't show up on Monday. I don't rush into the office, tired and pissed off, because I'm afraid of feeling guilty for not being there. My team has learned to recognize it as one of my strengths, because that means I've probably been working all day and night on Sunday. At some offices, the team would look at that and wonder what I was up to, but since I've clearly set parameters to my working style, they aren't looking around asking why Ryan isn't in on Monday. They know damn well I put in sixteen hours on Sunday, or I needed the day away to think.

As an entrepreneur, you should design your company around your personality and try to find people who accept that personality and can work with it.

I recently had to part ways with an attorney we used for my estate with whom I argued all the time. He was really good at what he did, but our work styles and personalities didn't match. As the client, I like to have my voice heard and have the person say something to the effect of, "Got it. Let me do my job, and I'll get you the best result." Instead, this lawyer liked to go over every detail of every point I made and argue about everything just to prove to me that he was right. Even if he was right, it didn't matter. I didn't hire an attorney to argue with me; I hired an attorney to argue with other attorneys, on my behalf. So I had to find a lawyer who was equally as good, but whose working style wasn't a problem. She could be like, "Ryan, would you mind? I'm the expert here." That's all she would have to say, and I'd shut the hell up.

I'm not big on formalities at ViSalus. I'll never forget the time I walked into the headquarters of Sirius XM, a multibillion-dollar-plus company, and everyone had full-sleeve tattoos, and Howard Stern and Seal were hanging around the place. I thought to myself, *You can own a multibillion-dollar company that is still the coolest place in the world to work.* Fuck the formalities. Good manners are important, and so are the traditional processes that are vital to running a successful company, but I refuse to work in a suit-and-tie culture that isn't designed around optimizing talent.

At ViSalus, I put a gym in our Michigan office, so technically we pay the employees of ViSalus to work out. We run the company this way because that's how I live my life, and how our co-founders live theirs. I know that if you're sitting at your desk all day snacking and feeling fat, your vitality will suffer, and so will your work. If someone tells me they're going to be in at 10 a.m. because they have to drop off their kid in the morning and then go to the gym, I know that they are optimizing themselves. And optimized workers get shit done.

After we sold ViSalus to Blyth, we had a lot more people involved in our day-to-day processes, and because we didn't conform to the standards of corporate America, they judged us. The friction became obvious after the damage had already been done. Learn from our mistake: If you find yourself deeply modifying the way you act around your team, it's not a good sign.

The point is, the company is you—it's your signature. As CEO, you literally sign the checks. No one else. The first part of becoming a rock star at what you do is taking responsibility for your career and figuring out your strengths and weaknesses; the second half is making sure everyone around you is cool with it.

CHAPTER 11
THE WRONG KIND
OF SUCCESS

Having started my career in the late '90s in the tech industry, I got to witness the first dot-com companies rise to prominence, minting many billionaires along the way. Netscape went public, Jeff Bezos raised hundreds of millions of dollars, Microsoft's stock created a massive multibillion-dollar fortune for Bill Gates. This wasn't just about raising money through venture capitalists, this was about these rock star tech entrepreneurs obtaining the coveted three-letter acronym: IPO. Initial public offering.

From the second I started my career as an entrepreneur, I dreamed about taking a company public. I wanted to ring the bell on Wall Street as a testament to my success and to cement my entrepreneurial prowess once and for all. The IPO is the biggest thing you can do as an entrepreneur. At least, so I thought.

The first time I actually believed it could happen was during a meeting with Bob Goergen, the CEO of Blyth, in April 2012. Blyth had purchased ViSalus in 2008, and since that time, my company had skyrocketed. We were making $65 million a month in sales, and were on track for $100 million in profit by the end of the year. Bob looked at me and simply said, "We can't pay you what we owe you. We've got to take the company public.

"You, Ryan, are going to become the CEO of a publicly traded company."

When I walked out of that meeting, I could have jumped ten feet in the air and punched a hole in the ceiling with my head. That's how ecstatic I was. I tried to assess the situation logically, not emotionally, but from that point forward, from April until August 2012, we completely changed our course—we were going public.

The plan was to make our announcement in August, right after a big company event called Vitality. We went into deep secrecy, because if word got out, it would impact Blyth's share price; they were already publicly traded. We had to make sure our security was tight and that none of our finances were leaked (there were already hedge funds calling to take me to lunch so they could learn more). We had to button up our compliance and hire attorneys. I shifted my entire focus from running a company to becoming the CEO of a public company. (That was a big mistake.)

When you take a company public, the way your valuation is determined is in comparison to your peers in the marketplace. ViSalus is a health and weight-loss company, so the question was, how did we compare to Weight Watchers or Herbalife? Herbalife, at that time, was trading at a multiple above everyone else. Because it's one of the few publicly traded companies in our industry, and the most similar to ViSalus, Herbalife became the benchmark to what we'd be valued at, and they were worth just north of a billion dollars. So, not only was I going to IPO a company, I was going to have the word "billion" next to my name ("billion-dollar entrepreneur" sounds sexy, doesn't it?). And although I wouldn't be making a billion dollars on the transaction, I sure as hell wanted to ring the bell on a billion-dollar IPO.

During our IPO preparation, we were listening in on the Herbalife quarterly conference calls, which we were very attuned to because we wanted to study and learn everything about them that we could—understand the analysts that covered them, the investors that invested in them—so we could be fairly positioned in our IPO launch. On one of these calls, a notorious short-seller named David Einhorn made a single request: "Explain to me how your sales model works."

Immediately Herbalife stock plunged double-digit percentages. As did Blyth's stock, and everyone else's in the direct-selling industry. All the investors that had been investing heavily in Herbalife had just jumped ship. They were thinking, "Oh no, David Einhorn is going to attack direct selling" (which he did not do). But what did happen is that David's actions alerted one of his short-seller buddies, Bill Ackman, to start shorting the stock. So, as a result of David Einhorn, the multiples of Herbalife dropped considerably—as did the valuation of my company. Our billion-dollar dream would soon get a rude awakening.

We proceeded cautiously, thinking seriously about our operations. We had to make sure our company was completely buttoned up. The short-sellers were coming—we didn't know how or when, but we knew they were coming for us. I could almost feel them the way surfers must be able to sense sharks, circling under the water. We decided to catch the wave anyway.

The Trap

It was August 2012, in the middle of the ViSalus IPO road map, when I was summoned to Wachtel, the most prestigious law firm in New York, for a meeting. I strode into the boardroom, flanked by a team of no fewer than six lawyers. I had never lawyered up this hard before. On one side of the room sat six Wall Street bankers, each with his own version of a $500 haircut and an impeccably tailored $5,000 suit. On the other side of the room sat six board members from Blyth, the Goergens, and six more of their attorneys. I looked for Todd Goergen's face first—he was one of my few allies, and we made eye contact. He had told me that he had instructed everyone in the room to read my book, *Nothing to Lose*, prior to the meeting, so they'd know who they were dealing with.

I was on track to make $100 million in profit for Blyth already that year; by all rights I had created a $1.5 billion company.

Ernst & Young had just named me entrepreneur of the year. I was greeted with standing ovations at every speech I made. I was being interviewed left and right, I was on TV, I was featured in *Fortune* for my *New York Times* bestseller, on TechCrunch, and soon I was going to fulfill every wish that this kid from the streets had ever imagined—I was going to ring that bell on Wall Street and take my company public.

The bankers handed out glossy, beautiful investment books and flashed their $50,000 watches and $3,000 cufflinks. I said very few words before they started taking me through their pitch. When they were done with their presentation, the bankers slid a piece of paper across the table at me. It had a number on it: $70 million.

I told myself, *I'm not going to fucking smile. I'm not going to smirk. I'm unimpressed. This is just the start.*

I knew what was up; they were there to sell me. This is how the game is played. The bankers and venture capitalists take you through their pretty sales pitch, then they show you your number, and once you show your cards and they know you're excited, they start asking you for their compromises. This time they might say, "You can't sell your shares for one year." The next time, they might say, "We need to reduce the valuation."

I flashed back to my SkyPipeline days, when I sat in a very similar meeting during the final sale. That time, the attorneys slid a piece of paper over to me and it had nothing on it. Zero. They had completely fucked me out of my share, and I had to use blatant demands and threats to renegotiate a better deal. I told myself that I'd never get myself into a similar situation again. There were a lot of details that could make what looked like a great deal on the first draft, a bad deal on the tenth. I had learned my lesson.

Now I was sitting in a very similar situation, only in a much nicer boardroom, looking at a piece of paper with seven zeroes on it, telling myself, *Don't smile. I'm not going to fucking smile.* Meanwhile, somewhere in my mind I flashed into the future. I'm spraying champagne, making it rain, I'm buying mansions in the Hollywood Hills, and parachuting into the Olympics. *Poker face. Back to your poker face, Ryan. You haven't closed this deal yet. This is fake money, Monopoly money. Don't show them your excitement. You haven't cashed the check yet.*

I was sitting there in a T-shirt and jeans surrounded by an army of suits. I had dressed down on purpose. I had one strategy, and that was to make everyone in the room as uncomfortable as possible. I knew how to play poker. They wanted to convince me that I only had a couple of jacks when I knew I was holding a royal flush. The meetings continued, and the compromises they requested multiplied. All those $5,000-an-hour lawyers' fees were piling up. Everyone was hanging on my every move, waiting for me to approve the transaction, but I wouldn't let them see my hand until I saw theirs.

Every time we met they dangled that $70 million carrot in front of me. Didn't I want to be the CEO of a public company? Didn't I want to be on the NYSE? My ego was screaming at me— *Close the fucking deal!* I had it all planned out in my mind. I reserved our ticker symbol VI. I had even picked out the outfit I was going to wear the day I would go ring that bell. This was the dream. But for some reason I just couldn't pull the trigger. All I could think was that my career was on the line. If the deal went wrong, it was my employees who would get hurt, my financial future that would suffer, and I'd be the villain, the one who left my new investors and shareholders holding the bag while everyone else at the table was cashing out. My goal was to do what I was doing for the rest of my life, not capitalize on one deal that fucked everyone else.

For every one time I've made the right decision in my career, there are another hundred times where I've let my ego and my impatience get the best of me. Times when I've had a quick win, and made a few million bucks and then relaxed and spent it all. Or I launched a product at the wrong time. Or trusted the wrong people. You get the point; I had made enough mistakes to realize that this IPO could be one of my biggest.

The bankers continued to push me to close the deal, they pushed my partners, and they pushed Blyth—and it wasn't hard, because everybody wanted to get rich. If they'd just have come clean with me and said, "Look, Ryan, we're going to make $10 million off this deal, and this is what we want," as opposed to saying, "Ryan, this is the best deal for *you*," I might have signed on the dotted line. But I was smart enough to know a sales pitch when I heard one. Every time they covered their true interests by baiting my ego, I trusted them less.

The truth was I was being offered the ego gratification of having a public company and a paper worth of over $70 million, when I was actually due $70 million in cash at the end of the year. They knew that, and now I knew it, too, but they underestimated me. (I guess they didn't read my book.)

In *Nothing to Lose* I wrote about my days in Juvenile Hall and how "nobody steals my milk." In jail the new guys always get tested to see how tough they are. They were always watching your reactions—what would you do if someone bumped into you in the hallway? Or what would happen if someone came over and asked for your milk during lunch? Would you jump up and fight, or would you hand it over meekly? I was a skinny white kid, so I had to catch on quickly. Nobody stole my milk.

It's the same principle in business. Everyone knows that if you cave in and compromise the first time they test you, you aren't the real deal. Soon they'll be taking your milk every day, and so will everyone else. In the end I had to listen to my instincts, and my gut was telling me that these people were trying to steal my milk. I went from holding myself back from smiling in triumph to restraining myself from shouting out, "You're trying to manipulate me, you fucking bankers."

That's the thing about negotiating nine-figure deals; they'll only tell you about the reward, not the trap. You're like an animal being hunted; if you're a smart animal, you'll hold back from making a move until you've seen the trap. You might be able to snatch the bait without falling in, or you might avoid the trap altogether. But if you don't see the trap, and you go walking in—whether you're raising money, ringing the bell on Wall Street, acquiring a company, or being acquired—the next thing you know, you're fucked. You might get snared career-wise when you really need to act, you might get financially killed, or caged for life.

By September 2012, after no fewer than fifty meetings, the trap had become apparent.

Hell No, IPO

My plan for the end of September was to buy a penthouse in Manhattan, take my company public, ring the NYSE bell, and build a firm that would operate by the rules of Wall Street, increase shareholder value, and make me a king. The IPO was scheduled for the third week of September; we had already notified our employees, filed our SI, and made headlines—the stock price of our parent company, Blyth, was skyrocketing, and I owned over $20 million worth of that too. After the IPO I was planning to fly back to LA and tie up some loose ends before I moved. With one decision my entire life would change.

After countless hours of back-and-forth deliberation, I canceled the IPO. I couldn't ignore what my gut was telling me, that the IPO would have been a disaster. This was the hardest internal business decision I had ever made. The next day, September 24, 2012, I spent the entire day on the phone. Blyth and the bankers begged me to reconsider, but I stood my ground. By the twenty-sixth they had to release the news. I watched my Blyth stock plummet; it dropped from $60 a share to $20 a share (I sold at $8 years later). In one second I'd wiped out tens of millions of my own personal net worth with no plan, and no support from my investors. All I had was doubt, lots of doubt.

Everyone except for my ViSalus cofounders told me I had made the wrong decision. While I had tens of millions in Blyth stock, my responsibility was to ViSalus shareholders, so I had to make the right decision for ViSalus. Nick and Blake understood my loyalties, and they were literally the only ones backing me.

I walked into a meeting with Blyth CEO Bob Goergen. He looked like a gambler who had just lost all his chips. "You cost me sixty million dollars," he said. "But what's sixty million dollars among friends?"

There was a hard edge in his voice that stopped me. His delivery was nothing short of angry and justified. I had to bite my tongue and calmly tell him that in a few years he'd be thanking me and telling me that I made the right decision. But at that moment, I knew he didn't see it. I understood his position. If someone had just cost me $60 million, they'd get a similar lashing from me. I had let my idol down. He was my mentor, and I respected the fact that I had impacted his plan and his agenda, and I had just cost him a lot of money. But I also knew that I'd played my hand correctly and in the end it was the right decision.

My face felt hot; it must have been completely red. We stared at each other in silence for a few moments. It was tense. Finally, I said, "Let's agree to disagree."

Bob gave me a look that I'll never forget—like nobody had ever said such a thing to him before. I can still feel the sting.

Vindicated

After we canceled the IPO, and I had that very, very difficult meeting with Bob, I had some very difficult meetings with the banks, and then some very difficult meetings with employees (some of whom were only on board for the IPO). It was dark days. Then in December, Bill Ackman made an announcement that not only was he taking a billion-dollar short position against Herbalife, he was making it his life's mission to destroy their company. I was completely vindicated.

I cited market conditions as the reason why we had canceled, but more than that, I knew Einhorn and his sharks were out there, underneath us, circling. My friends had been getting calls from private investigators, asking for information about some of the relationships I had with certain individuals. There had been some short-selling reports about Blyth and their relationship with me and my cofounders. It was a nasty, nasty feeling.

In retrospect, we shouldn't have entertained the idea of going public; we weren't ready for it. As it was, we had to weather terrible media and bad PR, all as a result of the "Bill Ackman period." Herbalife had crashed when I would have gone public, and we would have drawn more attention from the short-sellers. In other words, I wouldn't have a company today if I had taken it public. I'm still paying the price for my mistake, though. If I had said to Bob during that first meeting, "No way, we're not ready," who knows? We might have ended up with an even stronger company than the one we have now.

Watch This

At the end of 2012, I was at a Christmas party when I got a text from one of my hedge fund friends with a link to a video. "I want you to look at this video," he said. I didn't open it. When my friends send me videos, I'm always wary about clicking on them. For one thing, I don't want any viruses on my device. Second, if you have friends like mine, you're accustomed to getting unpleasant surprises. After asking him why he wanted me to click on the link, he said, "You have to look at this video. Just look at it."

Thinking it might be important I watched the video. It was a short-seller talking about all the massively successful shorts he had made that year. My friend is a hedge fund manager, so I assumed he had a part in creating the video. At the very end of the five-minute video came the grand finale: footage of me, walking on stage, about to give a speech, followed by the story of how Blyth stock declined, and how much profit resulted because of the short that this guy had put on it.

I canceled our IPO, and now I was the fodder for all these successful shorts on Blyth stock. I was the poster boy because of the decision I had made. All I could think was, *fuck them. They won this time.*

Back to the Hustle

My Blyth contract was up on December 31, 2012, and I was in a good position to negotiate. I had a strong company; we had made 54 percent of Blyth's sales that year. They couldn't raise the money they owed me, and I knew they didn't have it. I had leverage, but instead of using it, I made a commitment to the Goergens that I would not bend them over and force them to pay me all at once. I would find a deal that was equitable for both sides. While honorable in my intentions, I did have to ask myself if they would have done the same for me had they been in my position. The answer was yes.

I moved from Detroit back to Los Angeles. I had just bought my dream house with the money I thought I was going to make from the IPO. I stood in the living room of that stark, glass-and-steel, multimillion-dollar mansion, looking out over the expanse of the Hollywood Hills, thinking to myself, *I have to figure something out quick.* At that moment, I couldn't afford that home. I couldn't even afford to furnish it.

I decided to hire the best compensation consultants to negotiate my deal. One of my good friends, another hedge fund manager, went out of his way to find me the best. After rigorous meetings with every elite Wall Street attorney in the world, by December 2012 we had come to an agreement, and I signed. Blyth would give a significant amount of money to the ViSalus shareholders, the field members, and myself. Their last payment due was $248 million. I immediately went out and bought a Ferrari 458 Italia with cash, as a reward for getting the deal done, and parked it in the showroom-style garage at my home in the Hollywood Hills that I could now afford to live in. Sitting on your cash and looking at it every day in the bank does nothing for you, so I parked some of my money in houses, starting with the ones right next to me. I bought four multimillion-dollar homes as investment properties. I bought a Bombardier Challenger 300 private jet (because it had the name "challenger" in it). Then I went and bought myself $500,000 in watches. I splurged. Spending a few million on yourself when you've just made $56 million isn't so bad, I told myself. Plus, that was only a year's worth of hard work, and I had plenty more years left in me.

The more stuff I acquired, the more stressed I became. People started coming to my house to get me to sign their copies of *Nothing to Lose*. I'd have people showing up at all hours, and some of them were definitely characters; I had to put up a security perimeter. I now had to worry about my art collection, my watch collection, and my jet. With six cars and four homes I had to hire a fleet manager, and a full-time property manager. Every fucking day something had to be fixed somewhere, let alone the insurance I was paying for all the shit I had bought ($10,000 a month). And then of course there's my wardrobe. I needed a stylist to help me pull clothes and rotate them so I wasn't ruining them, and God forbid a moth should get into my $50,000 sweater collection. Disaster. Then I realized that I only had a 2012 Ferrari, and the new car smell had already worn off; it was almost time to buy a new one. And then it came to me—*fuck, I created an empire out of having nothing to lose, and now I've accumulated all these things that are destroying that very mind-set. I had gone from nothing to lose—to everything to lose.*

During a prayer one night I asked myself, "What would my stepfather Bob do?"

CHAPTER 12

WORK BACKWARD

The biggest war against ViSalus had actually happened way before we canceled the IPO. Back in early 2012, we were doing $65 million a month in sales. We felt unstoppable. On March 27, 2012, the news broke: A JetBlue pilot had had an apparent psychotic break during one of their routine flights from Las Vegas. He ran up and down the aisle screaming at terrified passengers, "Say your prayers—we're going down!"

As the crew scrambled to make an emergency landing, four passengers, including one former NYPD officer, locked the pilot out of the cockpit and restrained him. Someone later got a video of him being escorted off the plane and posted it on the Internet. Eyewitnesses said the deranged pilot had been shouting incoherently about Iran, Iraq, and Al-Qaeda. The public speculated. *Was he a terrorist? A terrorist sympathizer? Was he insane?* The media wheels started churning. Reporters dug up the pilot's last social media post for clues about his motivations and his behavior. His last tweet was him re-tweeting me—yours truly. He was one of our ViSalus promoters. (Fuck!)

This was an extinction event for any company. Not only was I not unstoppable—I had just been stopped.

The media jumped all over it. *Could it be the ViSalus products that caused his mental breakdown? Good Morning America* immediately brought in experts and doctors who began blaming ViSalus products and talking about all the theoretical harm they could cause. Was it the caffeine? Are they a cult? Is this a fad diet?

I was sitting there—and I still get chills just thinking about it—watching my empire crumble right in front of me on the screen, while a bunch of speculating TV doctors accused us of being a public-safety hazard. It wasn't true, but the fact that the public now believed that our products might be hazardous was all that mattered. And our competitors smelled blood in the water.

I spent that entire night pacing around my apartment in Detroit, talking to crisis PR people, pilots, and my own employees, trying to determine what the facts were in this situation. My legal team immediately began to threaten legal action against news outlets and anyone else who impugned the safety of our products. Meanwhile, our competition started spreading rumors that the National Transportation Safety Board and Food and Drug Administration had found rat poison in our products (which, of course, they don't contain). In response to this, even more of our competitors picked up their pitchforks and were screaming that our products were killing people. Then the Wall

Street short-sellers jumped into the fray and immediately started commissioning investigative reports and hiring private detectives to find any hole in our company to support their short on Blyth's stock. It was a nightmare. Every time we plugged one hole in the dam, another would gush open. It dragged on for days. I felt like I was losing my mind.

The pilot was involuntarily hospitalized and closely monitored. In the meantime, JetBlue's pilots' union released a message to their crew: No pilots were allowed to use ViSalus products. Apparently, many of them were customers.

Something came over me; it was like a survival instinct. I started compartmentalizing. In the chaos I could only focus on my next exact response, my next move, and nothing else. I wanted to see the pilot's auto-ship records, to determine which products he had been using, whether these products had been in our warehouse, and if he was using any other products from other companies. Were there any other social media posts that would indicate abnormal behaviors or affiliations? We searched for any detail, anything that could help me turn this nightmare around.

Two weeks after the pilot was admitted to the psych ward, he had another psychotic episode. And this time it was in front of a judge. He was clean of any products from my company that he might have had in his system, which proved that there had been no correlation to ViSalus. Our name was cleared; it was a huge relief. But this event had created the first crack in the foundation that would someday crumble and cost us hundreds of millions of dollars in lost sales. The damage was done.

Now, I know what you're probably thinking—it was an uncontrollable event. In my opinion, it wasn't. If I could go back in time, I'd have been better prepared for it. When you're just starting to fly high, you think you're never going to come down, but God has a way of humbling you when you least expect it (and most deserve it).

The Worst-Case Scenario

Over dinner at a steakhouse in Manhattan—about five martinis in—the CEO of Jefferies Group, Richard Handler, once told me I should read every *Wall Street Journal* exposé on every CEO indicted in recent history, and every article on SEC problems, deals gone wrong, and partnership breakups. It was great advice.

Business is all about learning from your big mistakes and the mistakes of others. Having gone through the JetBlue incident and lawsuit after lawsuit, now when I'm initiating any new venture, along with thinking about the best thing that could happen, I also think to myself: What's the worst thing that can happen?

I've had former employees sue me for bogus reasons. Sometimes people will even lie about you. I've had two class-action lawsuits. I've had to settle out of court like a lot of companies do because it wasn't worth the attorney's fees to pursue the suits, even though they were based on lies. I have spent no less than

$10 million in attorneys' fees just because of my success. Sometimes I want to fight the lawsuits, but it just costs too much. *What's the worst that could happen? Could I go bankrupt?* (I already know the pain of that, so it's not the worst thing that could happen, but it sucks.)

Ever since my earliest days as an entrepreneur, when I'm faced with a potentially volatile situation, my first reaction is to shut the door and get everyone away from me until I have clarity on the issue. I don't go absolutely radio silent, but I drop to about 10 percent availability because I need to think through every scenario I possibly can. I need to overwhelm myself with those scenarios until I've eliminated a number of them and stack-ranked the rest from highest probability to lowest probability. Then I figure out the most likely scenario and work backward from there. Most entrepreneurs make the mistake of reacting emotionally under pressure and grabbing the first solution that looks like a life raft. I don't do that. I've learned to work backward from the worst-case scenario, bank on the most likely scenario—and leave my hopes for the "best case" because, in all likelihood, it isn't going to happen.

At War

One of my favorite quotes attributed to Winston Churchill is: "If you're going through hell, keep going." I first heard it from a friend, Rich Riley, the CEO of Shazam, when ViSalus was going through a difficult time after we canceled the IPO. At the time, I had brought him onto the board of directors to help me talk some sense into Blyth. We were deep in our many issues and he could sense I wanted to throw in the towel. What he delivered to me was magic! The quote has stuck with me ever since.

Churchill had his flaws, but he pushed back against Nazi Germany when others wouldn't. He created a strategy, influenced allies, and, thank God, won the war. As entrepreneurs there will be times when absolutely everything is going to look negative to you, but I'm guessing that whatever your "hell" is, it's probably not as bad as "Nazi Germany hell." So, keep going. Even the toughest wars can be won, as long as you believe in what you're fighting for.

When I was a gang member, we were constantly at war. We were at war with rival gangs, with ourselves, with our families, with the police, and with poverty. It is the same with business—you're at war with direct competitors, indirect competitors, yourself, and even technological changes. If you look at some of the countless businesses that didn't fight their wars correctly, you can learn some valuable lessons.

Take ViSalus's competitor Weight Watchers, for example. This was at one time a $2 billion-plus company. They were pioneers, developing and selling a diet program technology that counted points. Then tools such as MyFitnessPal, Fitbit, and even the Apple Watch came along, and suddenly, this technology was free. A single technological change completely killed the Weight Watchers business model. Their high-to-low valuation looked something like $1.8 billion to less than $300 million, in less than two years. Weight Watchers had to let their CEO go, and then hired a rock star spokeswoman, Oprah, to get back in the game.

That's how fast it can happen if you don't have the right "at war" mind-set or the right strategy in place. The speed of innovation is a war in itself.

Hopefully you'll never have to face anything as intense as what ViSalus faced with JetBlue, or Weight Watchers faced with their technology challenge, but if you want to be a great leader, or lead a great company, you're going to be battle tested. Each war you'll fight is a battle test. And the bigger your success, the more formidable your competitors, and the bigger target you become.

What does a battle test look like in business? It's someone stealing from you. Someone lying. Somebody spreading rumors behind your back, or sabotaging your operations. Sometimes, the war is even with your own employees, or with the culture of your company. I have a lot of firsthand experience with this type of war. It's a silent type of war, and you don't even know you're in one until you've already lost.

Between 2010 and 2012, when we went from seventy employees to five hundred employees in less than two years, our company's culture changed radically. We had the happy misfortune of having to rapidly hire people for positions that were being created every day. In good times, you attract people who like a "good times ride." Also, our tendency as humans is to hire people who are like us—and that includes people who share our weaknesses. When ViSalus was doing $97 million in profit in 2012, it was really fun around the office. The easiest job in the world is when you have tons of money coming in and your job is to spend it. After a while, with the combination of the wrong people with the wrong cultural values making the wrong decisions again and again, you've got a disaster on your hands. Some companies go out of business because of this. We cared too much to let that happen.

In 2012 we had plenty of money in the bank, but our best-selling product, the Vi-Shake, was under attack. After the Jet-Blue incident, our competitors had begun spreading rumors that our shakes were killing people, and had successfully created a perceived weakness in the product. Our billion-dollar product had begun to flounder in the marketplace. We had the wrong soldiers under the wrong generals (myself included), and a series of bad internal decisions ensued—a lot of decisions I wouldn't make today, in retrospect.

After some intense meetings, we decided to pivot, and I confidently marched the entire company into the field with a brand-new product—cereal. Unfortunately, this wasn't a perfect solution (not that any solution is ever perfect). Of course we had made a product we could be proud of, and our cereal is the best cereal on the market, but as a result, we had to price it very high and this challenged consumers' preconceived ideas of how much a cereal should cost—98 percent of all households have cereal in them, and 98 percent of households think they know how much cereal should cost. Our cereal brought in $20 million in sales, but it wasn't the $1 billion we had hoped for.

In retrospect, we should have just focused on reinventing

our shake. Unlike with cereal, most households don't already have a shake in them, and therefore we can ask for a premium for a product that is of the highest quality without challenging any of our consumers' expectations. During key meetings, certain team members advised against "cannibalizing" our shake product, which was the solution that we actually needed. If I had known better, we'd have seen this. But I didn't know what I didn't know.

Shortly after this misstep, I looked around and said to myself, I'd rather have fewer employees making better decisions—knowing what I don't know—instead of hundreds of employees learning from mistake after mistake.

We began the worst set of layoffs I've ever experienced. We laid off hundreds of people during the first round, and another fifty or so during the next one. I had to let go of good people along with the bad, and I cried more than once after someone left my office. The most miserable feeling in the world is telling wave after wave of people who depend on you that they no longer have a job because you failed them as a leader.

The truth is wars never stop. Your competitors will continue to find weaknesses in your strategies, and exploit them. Unethical people will still target your company with lies and lawsuits, and the media will always have more of an agenda to sell the news than it does to report the truth. And the same ones that build you up will swiftly tear you apart.

Slow Your Roll

If you have a company that sells $36 million one year, $231 million the next, and more than $600 million the following year, like we did, you'll find yourself in a comfort zone, and that's the worst place to be. When you're hot, it's too easy to lose perspective. When a company suddenly shoots up, there's high fives all around, and you're getting rich. You're so high, and you want to see how high you can go. And eventually the air gets thin.

Growth is what Wall Street values the most. If you ever want to get rich, take your company public, or sell it for far more than the revenue you produce, then you have to demonstrate growth. Month over month, quarter over quarter, year over year. Growth is why you've raised the money in the first place. It's the reason why Facebook is worth $350 billion (at the time of the publication of this book), because they expect it to grow.

As start-up entrepreneurs we craved growth at all costs. But what they don't tell you in business school is that growth can cost you your company, because growing out of control without the right processes in place will break you down. In business, "You're either in control, or you're out of control."

When ViSalus started growing fast, we looked for outside mentorship, and I flew out my entire executive team to meet Tony Hsieh and attend a few meetings to learn about some of the best practices of Zappos, which is a phenomenal company. At one point during the Q and A with Tony, I told him that we were on target to grow by 350 percent that year. He looked shocked. If you've ever met Tony Hsieh you'll notice that he's a very analytical person, and it's rare to get a lot of expression out of him.

Tony said, "If I was on your board I would tell you to slow down your growth."

It was my turn to look shocked. I remember thinking that was the stupidest idea in the world. *I have worked my whole life to create a profitable company with real growth, and you want me to slow it down?*

"It's impossible to slow down growth—what should I do, tell my sales force to quit selling?" I said.

In a low monotone, Tony said, "You could raise prices. That would slow down your growth."

At that point in time we were just about to sell a billion dollars' worth of shakes, and take the number one market share for meal replacement shakes in North America, so I figured our price points must be working. But I didn't say that.

Tony must have been reading my mind. He said, "Growth covers a lot of mud."

I read an interview with Yahoo CEO Marissa Mayer in which she talked about her early days at Google. When Eric Schmidt joined the team in 1999, he originally shot down Google's plan to double its size from two hundred employees to four hundred. He was convinced they wouldn't be able to keep their standard of quality and their culture if they diluted it across a larger workforce. He only let the company hire fifty new people for the entire year, which was difficult but forced them to prioritize when hiring.

Marissa's comment was, "Hypergrowth is fun, but you have to be careful."

Looking back, I should never have allowed the company to "hypergrow" the way it did. If I had to do it over again, I'd have raised prices immediately. Delayed shipments. Anything. It would have spread the growth out over a few years. If I could go back in time, I'd have taken 20 percent growth in 2012, another 20 percent in 2013, and so on, and in the end I'd probably be worth $100 million more than I am today—had I done that. Tony was right, growth covers mud—when the tide pulled back on ViSalus's growth, I was knee-deep in mud.

CHAPTER 13

WHO DO YOU WORK FOR?

One time, at 24x7 Tech, my first start-up, my business partner approached me after I made some business decisions that he apparently disagreed with. He told me, "Ryan, I've given you a long leash, but I'm afraid I'm going to have to pull it now."

His analogy was so vivid, I remember thinking to myself, *One . . . fuck you, I'm not a dog. Two, I'm not a true entrepreneur. Not if this asshole thinks there's a leash around my neck that he can pull on.* This realization led me to sell 24x7 Tech immediately.

All entrepreneurs desire autonomy. We crave it. That's what drives a lot of us to quit our jobs and start our own companies. Every leader needs a degree of autonomy to make the right decisions, but the thing about autonomy in business is, you have to ask for it—nobody is ever going to hand it to you. And once you have it, rest assured, someone will try to take it away from you.

Today, I have levels of autonomy and self-governance built into all my business environments. I go days not talking to people sometimes. I've noticed that some people will take advantage of it—I'm the best boss ever, the boss who never calls you—and other people will panic if I disappear for a few days while I'm sorting things out in my mind. People fear what they don't know, and if they don't have a similar need for autonomy, your ability to work on a project alone may scare them.

The irony is that when you're in good times, autonomy is given freely, and in rock-bottom times, it's not. But you need it the most in crisis moments, when you need the freedom to take risks, listen to your gut, and solve problems on your own. I demand it with every business venture I go into now, because otherwise other people can overrule my decisions or my instincts as an entrepreneur.

You don't have to leave your company (or get forced out) to get autonomy. But you have to basically become so good at what you do that they'll give you autonomy just to keep you; and this isn't an assumed or an implied autonomy—it must be in writing in your contract that you have a right to it.

In the movie *The Big Short*, Christian Bale's character, Michael Burry, is on the phone with his investors and he is 100 percent concrete on the decision he's made to short the housing market. In one scene the investors are freaking out on him. Burry says something like, "In my contract, I have full autonomy to make these decisions." He had to invoke his contractual right to autonomy to keep his investors at bay. It turns out it was one of the most profitable trades in the history of Wall Street, and it wouldn't have happened if he had not had autonomy in his contract. Later in an interview, Burry said that some of his investors were still mad at him to this day for enforcing his autonomy, even after he had made them lots of money.

Once you're an absolute rock star, and you've earned the right to make decisions on your own (and secured independence in your contract), you need to maneuver around people who will stunt your autonomy as you build your business. But, on the other hand, to be a true partner you can't always seek autonomy as your first priority. I don't think any person running a business has *full* autonomy. And a big part of doing business is maintaining relationships with investors, shareholders, and business partners.

For example, nobody is going to tell me, in my role as a CEO, to do something I disagree with doing, but I may get told to do something that I haven't yet made a priority. It happens all the time. I treasure and seek autonomy, so I tend to give it left and right to my team, which isn't always the best way to manage. Technically, the opposite of being an employee is having autonomy, and there are some employees who should not have absolute autonomy. Some people thrive on structure; others wake up every day with enough desire to do their job without having to be told to do it. And then there are some people who crave autonomy so much that they will refuse a perfectly good suggestion, just so they can exercise their freedom. When I see somebody doing something solely out of principle instead of logic, I try to stay away from them. If you can, I recommend you do the same.

Don't Break Up the Band

After Blyth bought Vi, we had anything but autonomy. It came to a breaking point one night when all three of us quit in an e-mail chain. I started it, but it wasn't the first time I tried to resign. Nick responded a while later with: "I quit." And then Blake responded with the same line—and Blake doesn't throw those words around. Ever.

After I saw Blake's resignation, I thought, *Oh shit!* My resignation was dependent on them running the company, and was thereby retracted.

Of course, we weren't quitting. We couldn't quit ViSalus. I was paid not to quit. I made over $10 million that year, but I wasn't happy. For me, happiness and autonomy go hand in hand. We were tired of playing by Wall Street's rules. I was constantly pushing back against the board. The structure of the company was killing any of the passion the three of us had left for our business. And the board was beginning to see that they wouldn't win by increasing their oversight. It was time to change.

ViSalus needed to be relieved of Wall Street. Publicly, we were attacked, derided, and dismissed. We needed to be able to rally around every victory rather than have the successes of our promoters and staff devalued by a biased outsider's perspective.

I struggled with this idea, the Goergens were like family to me, and I didn't want to hurt them. But clearly the liability they were carrying called "ViSalus" was hurting their business. Their stock price was plummeting. At that time, they owed us $148 million, their stock had gone from $45 to $5 during this period, and their company was worth less than they owed us.

In one of the many conversations I had with Bob Goergen, he shared one of his formulas that he learned at McKinsey, and carried with him into his many businesses. The lesson was this: When you have a problem, it's people, structure, or process.

After Bob had delivered that piece of wisdom, I went and thought about it. I spent many hours thinking about how to solve my problem. I thought, *Is it a people issue?* Nick, Blake, and I love the company, and we love the employees, our customers, and promoters, and we're all smart people. We make mistakes, but we do get better. So, it couldn't be a people issue.

As a result of scaling the business we had put thousands of processes in place; we even had a project management department just to manage all the processes. I doubted that we were one step-by-step process away from success. Adding more processes wasn't the problem—so it had to be the structure.

Structural issues are tricky, because if you have good people with the right process under a bad structure, those people won't be able to perform. The bad structure prevents good processes from being created and good people from creating. So, we had to change our structure.

Then I had an epiphany. I was dissecting our internal structures, debating on whether to move people from our Michigan headquarters to Europe when I realized that maybe *I* was the one in a bad structure. It occurred to me—the whole Blyth deal in itself was a bad structure.

Getting into a bad structure is like getting into a bad relationship—it happens over time. If you had known you were getting into a bad marriage, you wouldn't have gotten engaged in the first place. That's what happens with structure; as the years go by decisions get made and more and more compromises start to pile up. When we had sold the company to Blyth, Nick, Blake, and I didn't know we wanted to work with each other for the rest of our lives. All we saw was an opportunity to get rich. I don't regret a single thing, because I learned so much, but in retrospect we probably shouldn't have made that deal with Blyth.

I was in a quandary, because Blyth owed Blake, myself, and Nick $105 million of the $148 million they owed us. But I knew the present state of ViSalus and with Blyth's declining stock price, they might not be around to pay it anyway if I didn't do a deal. In essence we were owed $105 million, but what good was it if we weren't going to get paid? I thought to myself, *We have already been paid over $100 million. I have gotten as much as I'm ever going to get from this transaction.*

I met with Nick and Blake and discussed the idea of getting out from under Blyth; we decided to forgive their debt of $148 million, and they would give us a $6-million credit facility that we would match with our own cash. And we could announce the deal in as little as sixty days.

I said, "This is the right thing to do." But I didn't have to convince them. ViSalus is everything to them. Nick immediately said, "I'm in. Thirty-four million dollars, no problem." The hit of losing the future payout of more than $34 million was not insubstantial. It wasn't pocket change; it represented a large percentage of our wealth. But we believed we would see that money eventually, or die trying.

After I had gotten clarity during one of my week-long autonomy sessions, I went to Bob and said, "I think I know what our problem is."

I told him that we had made a series of decisions, and put a structure in place with them that wasn't working. "We gotta change it," I said.

For the first time in my career I was speaking Bob Goergen's language.

After I had gotten that off my chest, I jumped on a plane to meet the Goergens in their house in the Hamptons, to talk about how we had gotten to this place and how we'd get out of it. I had never been to the Hamptons before, and it was a warm summer day. I watched the scenery from inside of a dark air-conditioned town car, thinking I was going to the Hamptons not to have fun and party, the way I'd always dreamed, but to part ways with Blyth.

It was an eerie feeling sitting in the room with them that day. If I pulled this trigger, I would no longer have a safety net. I would no longer have the credentials of being an officer of a publicly traded company. *Time* magazine would no longer be giving me accolades for how much money I earned. But, there would be no scrutiny from Wall Street. Or the excuse of Blyth. I would no longer be putting hundreds of hours into my board presentations—I would no longer even have a board.

This wasn't just a divorce; it was a complete identity rethink.

I had been lying to myself for seven years—the most important years of my career—and operating under a structure that I now clearly saw as a detriment.

I told Blyth I wanted my company back. More attorneys, more bankers, more meetings, and finally, on September 4, 2014, Nick, Blake, and I enacted our plan. We bought ViSalus back from Blyth for $148 million, which was a fraction of what we sold it for, but about three times what we should have paid. I wasn't pushing all my chips in, but $34 million was still a lot of chips to push in. There was enough pressure to put me back in a nothing-to-lose mind-set—the place from where I know how to fight best.

We now owned 90 percent of the company and Blyth owned 10 percent. We eliminated Blyth's obligation to us in return for majority ownership in the company. One of my conditions with the buyback was that there would be no board of directors. I was tired of answering to a group of people who were engaged for a day, had limited context for the advice they were offering, and whose main role was to hold me accountable on the numbers. I held myself more accountable to the numbers than they ever would, and if I lost my focus, I had two partners who would do it for me.

The day the deal was announced, I was literally partying my ass off. I invited some friends over and we were up late playing cards. I had forgotten that the news would hit the East Coast at 6 a.m. their time, which was 3 a.m. my time. I hadn't told any of my friends about this deal. All of a sudden I got an alert, the news had been released, and Blyth stock was skyrocketing. The headline read: Blyth Stock Skyrockets 40 percent, ViSalus Founders Buy Back Company.

I owned several hundred thousand shares of Blyth stock at the time—it was a nice little gain. But I knew that the money would go in one pocket and right out the other into ViSalus. After the deal, Blyth's investors didn't have much love for me. (I've been called the devil more than once.) But in that transaction, what they thought of me wasn't my concern.

The most important thing was I was a free man.

The Reality of Autonomy

But was I really free?

Three months after the buy back, I decided to take a weekend to work from home and brainstorm about the business. I like to get work done by the pool, so I was sitting there with my toes in the sand, looking over my schedule for the upcoming months. Normally, I plan my board meetings a year out, that way I can confirm all the attendees and plan accordingly. As I opened up my Outlook calendar, I saw a year's worth of board meetings with Blyth still on the books. I thought, *Wow! Not only am I not going to attend a board meeting for this quarter, but I don't have to attend another board meeting again.*

It was a bit scary. The amount of work necessary to effect change and turn a company around was far greater than we had anticipated and nothing that we had planned went according to plan. We'd replaced our board with ourselves—myself, Nick, Blake, and Todd—but was this right for the company? It dawned on me that without a strong board to hold us accountable, solve problems, and notice blind spots, we'd have to put structures in place to off-set our autonomy and fill in the gaps.

People often have misconceptions about what companies are. We see these gigantic logos on the sides of high-rise office buildings and we think that the company is the brand, the mission statement, or their products. Really, all it is, is a bunch of people working together under a legal structure, or a few legal structures. The reality of autonomy is, you're never really free in business because there are still a lot of people depending on you. In essence, you want a certain amount of autonomy in your company, but never absolute autonomy—otherwise you're a company of one.

Going Solo

Sometimes you may be so much of a rock star, you may find yourself with a whole new dilemma—*Should I go solo?*

Maybe you're at the top of your profession, and you love what you do, but you feel like you can't effect the kind of changes you'd like to see within the current system. Like when Kobe Bryant told the Lakers it was either Shaquille O'Neal or him, that he was going to leave the team if he couldn't be the leader. Or the group of people you're in just aren't playing to your strengths. Maybe they won't give you the autonomy you crave. You want to go solo and start a consulting practice or write about what you know, do things your own way.

Or maybe the environment you've found yourself in suddenly feels too comfortable. You don't have to work too hard at it, and that's a bad thing. All that energy that you had previously been putting toward work is now going toward solving your dilemma. *Should I start my own business? Should I go solo?*

Personally, I've faced this dilemma. I've found myself in the "comfort zone," with ViSalus before, and debated on whether or not to stick with it, start a new venture, or go solo. Today, I'm the CEO and single largest shareholder of ViSalus, working alongside my cofounders, Nick Sarnicola and Blake Mallen, and Todd Goergen, to rebuild the company we took to great heights only a few years back. For some reason, with this amount of pressure and uncertainty, I've found my sweet spot. Maybe it's because of the environmental conditions and adversity I grew up in, but I love being right where I'm at right now. This is my gift zone: impossible odds, the highest amount of stress, the biggest risks, the highest stakes. So when I think about selling my company—leaving, exiting, or maximizing my notoriety—I also know that either I'll be looking back with regret, thinking I'd wished I'd stayed, or looking back in gratitude for the challenges we overcame.

You've got about a fifty-fifty chance of making it on your own. Even the biggest rock stars have failed at their well-intentioned solo careers. You're either Mick Jagger sitting on four flopped solo albums before returning to the Rolling Stones, or you're Beyoncé, who I'm sure hasn't once looked back at the days of Destiny's Child and wished she'd stayed.

So, before you strike out on your own, here are some questions to help you organize your thoughts:

1. What type of solo artist are you? What are you looking to achieve, and why can't you find it in the environment you're in now?
2. Have you invested everything in what you're currently doing?
3. If you split, will it be based on personal motives, like a lack of chemistry between you and your "band"? Is this the smartest thing you can do for your career, or is this ego? Examine what's driving you, and be honest.
4. What if you make the jump, and you're wrong? What will you do?
5. What will your older self tell your younger self? Which is more likely, that you will regret not going for it when you had the chance, or that you'll wish you'd stuck with it?
6. Historically, are you better on your own, or are you the type of person who needs a band behind them?

The final answers to these questions can only come from you, because they're likely to be different for every person. But hopefully, if you find yourself someday faced with this dilemma of going solo, and you're considering making a big career-defining jump, these will be the questions that help you make the smartest decision possible.

Now that you understand the questions to ask, and you've made your decision, let's talk about playing at the next level.

CHAPTER 14
SO YOU WANNA BE A ROCK STAR

People from all around the world take their vacations in Los Angeles. They deliver them on tour buses, and dump them out by the scenic roadside of Mulholland Drive to snap photos of where I live, the Hollywood Hills. When I look out the window of my multimillion-dollar home, within eye sight, I can see three other homes that I own. A million dollars is an inconsequential number to me at this point in my life. Don't get me wrong, I still like making an extra million here and there, but it doesn't quite have the impact it once had. Living in LA has given me access to elite social circles of the entertainment industry. One of my best friends is a legitimate rock star. He made the mistake of telling me about how he and his bandmates like to trash hotel rooms when they're on tour. Not to be outdone, in his hotel room that night I showed him a whole new level of trashing a room. In the morning I got a bill for $15,000, and I barely dodged jail in the process. Another time, at my friend Terrence J.'s birthday party, I noticed the table next to us received sparklers and champagne. I ordered twenty thousand dollars' worth of Dom Pérignon and so many sparklers that the fire marshal had to shut down the club. It was totally worth it.

I have watches I haven't even worn in a year, and clothes in my closet with the tags still on them. I have a DJ booth in my house, even though I don't spin records. I had thirty tons of pure white sand hand delivered and installed next to my infinity pool, just so my friends and I wouldn't have to go to the beach. I have dated every type of actress, model, and musician I desired—I have every "trophy" on my mantel. Backstage passes to meet Madonna: check. Artist credentials: check. Lollapalooza: no problem. The *Forbes* list? It's gorgeous.

Do you hate me yet? This is ridiculous, isn't it? I've spent a million dollars on bottle service—how many kids could get a better education with that money?

I'm bragging here, because I have this life, but I'm not about this life. I might flaunt my cars a little, but you probably didn't know any of these things about me. You'll never see photos of me with a bunch of models in G-strings around my pool, or a pit bull wearing a gold watch, or me rolling around in stacks of cash. Even if I did do those things, it wouldn't be anybody's business. I've done everything a rock star has done, I've checked off all the boxes, but I've learned after wasting time, wealth, and a lot of brain cells—those boxes are empty.

Own Your Image

We live in a world of rock stars—where a lot of businessmen are celebrities, and a lot of celebrities are businessmen. We're obsessed with billionaires, and there's only a couple of thousand of them. Jay Z said it best: "I'm not a businessman. I'm a business, man." From the cars he drives to the alcohol he drinks to the music he listens to, even to the clothes he wears, it's all one brand. And based on his number thirty-eight *Forbes* celebrity ranking, he gets paid off everything he touches.

Growing up listening to a heavy dose of hip-hop and rap, I wanted to be just like that. Later, when I started looking for mentors in the business world, I didn't want just any mentor, I wanted mentorship from the guys on the covers of magazines. And those "guys" have the best-integrated empires. Jay Z, Puff Daddy, Russell Simmons, Beyoncé, and Rihanna—they're a combination of brand provocateur and business.

Like everyone with a hustler's ambition, I aspired to be like my early idols, so I set out to do the same as they did. My dilemma was how to go from a suit-wearing, briefcase-carrying businessman (who was secretly listening to rap) to creating a brand in business unique to myself—but without selling out.

It was 2004, I was sitting in my apartment in Marina Del Rey, my business was finally getting momentum, and I was working myself out of the hole. I used the Marina City Club not only as my residence, but I also took meetings there around the clock with anyone and everyone that I thought could help me.

At that time, I was obsessed with learning techniques from other motivational speakers, and I chose to study the very best at the profession: Tony Robbins. I would often interview his employees so that I could learn about him. In one such meeting with his number one sales producer, I had prepared a list of a hundred questions, like I do prior to every meeting, and one of my questions was: "What would you do if you were Tony Robbins?"

She said, "I would show my thorns."

I said something to the effect of, "What the fuck are you talking about?" The image in my head was of a thorny human being.

"You're a rose," she said. "We love roses, because they are beautiful and perfect. You're charismatic, well groomed, and polished, but you're too polished. You need to expose your thorns."

From that point forward I started to show my thorns. Because traditional businessmen don't expose their thorns, but real people do. And real people are rare these days. I decided I wasn't a traditional businessman, and transparency is a mandate. I took my skeletons out of the closet and put them in the bookstore, and now my best seller is my version of "rapping about yesterday." That was the first step in reinventing myself from businessman to brand. And it worked.

When I exposed my thorns—bankruptcy, ex-gang member, baby out of wedlock, convicted of a 211—I got a whole lot of people saying, "Hey, I've got those thorns, too." But I also got a hell of a lot of people who don't have as many thorns and had a lot of opinions on someone who does.

And for those people, the forthcoming playlist is dedicated to you.

Playlist for My Haters

I took my son to school the other day, and we were a little late, so I peeled out of my driveway quicker than usual in my Ferrari, and suddenly there was a cop behind me. I live in a very secluded (and steep) section of the Hollywood Hills, so seeing a cop up there is a rarity. He pulled me over right in front of my place. The first thing I thought was, *That's odd.*

As the cop got out of his vehicle, I noticed immediately that this was no ordinary police officer. He looked like one of the old gang-enforcement cops: a tall, well-built Latino man with slicked-back hair, wearing all black. I thought, *This guy's going to kill me.* He saw my son in the car when he walked up, and I could tell he changed his attitude a bit, so he wouldn't scare Reagan.

He asked me some general questions. I answered, addressing him as "sir." I have the utmost respect for our police force. My brother-in-law was formerly the chief of police, and I've had my home robbed before; I know that we need the police to protect us.

Then he said, "Please step out of the car."

As I got out of the car, I thought, *I'm getting arrested.* I started having a total flashback to my gang days. I knew how this was going to go down. I was thinking, *I'm going to jail. He's going to cuff me.* I might have been driving too fast, but unless I had done something really wrong, I shouldn't have been asked to step out of my car—not for a little excess speed. He then asked me to come over to the trunk of his car (where they arrest you). I saw my son with his cute little blue eyes peeping out at me; he'd crawled over to the driver's-side seat to see what was happening to Daddy.

The officer looked at him and said, "It's okay, son. Daddy and I are just talking."

Then he turned to me and said, "You're at war right now."

"What war?" I asked.

"War with your neighbors," he said.

The cop proceeded to tell me that my neighbors had told them that I had no respect for the police. They said I called the police "pigs." Nothing could be further from the truth. The truth was that the neighbors were upset that I was having events at my house all the time. I have social gatherings, work meetings, dinner parties, film shoots, photo shoots—all kinds of business and other events at my house. In fact, people in my company refer to me as the CEO—the Chief Entertainment Officer— because it's my job to entertain. So, because they are passive-aggressive, instead of calling me, my neighbors thought they could manipulate the police into doing their dirty work. This is where it went wrong for the neighbors.

"I know who you are. I've read your book," the officer said. "I've wanted to tell you for a long time that I'm proud of you. You are one of those people I tell kids on the street that they can be like. I pulled you over because I wanted to show the neighbors that I'm taking action, and I want to help you win this war with your neighbors."

Then he told me his story, how he overcame gang violence and became a police officer. He went from being a detriment to society to becoming an authority in our community. Next thing, we were shaking hands and agreeing on a strategy to win the war together. I went from thinking, *Oh my God, I'm getting arrested* to *Wow! I've done something that's made an impact on someone.*

My point is that if you continue to do good in life (and I'm not saying I'm at all perfect in this respect), it will have a ripple effect and will impact people. When you have a positive impact on people, those people will see through the bullshit, and if you find yourself the target of other people's maliciousness or jealousy, your people will have your back.

I have the most expensive pieces of property in my neighborhood, and if anything, I've done a lot to increase the value of every house on my street. But I guess some people don't see it that way. As I climbed back in my car, I waved at the cop and said, "Next time the neighbors complain, tell them I am happy to buy their houses, too!" But of course it didn't stop there.

One of my neighbors recently told my real estate agent that he suspected me of money laundering. He knows nothing about me. He just sees that I own several houses on his block, which is several more houses than he has, and he assumes I'm doing something illegal. This is what we call a "hater."

What he didn't know was that I bought the house next door to me because I like my privacy. I wanted my best friend, Matt Arnold, who's a prominent Hollywood writer and director, to move in next door. I told him I paid $1.75 million for it. I thought it was worth a lot more, but it needed some work. I offered to give him the house at exactly what I paid for it six months after I had bought it. He declined and now, eighteen months later, the house is worth $3 million. Jokingly he now asks if the offer is still on the table. The answer is no. I like my privacy.

So, now I'm the guy who not only has a bigger house than my neighbor, but who also owns the house next door to it, and that's so offensive that he had come up with something as ridiculous as money laundering to "explain" it. Not only that, but he actually went out of his way to tell other people the story. My neighbor has a perfectly nice house and, from what I know, a respectable job, too. But that's not enough for some people. They have to try to bring you down. Because it takes a man to build a house, and any jackass can tear one down.

When my first book, *Nothing to Lose, Everything to Gain*, came out, the short-sellers at Blyth killed me in blogs. They ridiculed me and tried to say I was hiding information about my background. One of them wrote that in my book I failed to mention that I had filed Chapter 11 bankruptcy. I said that I lost all my money, which to me is the equivalent of saying I filed, but to this guy, that wasn't enough. He had to see the words "Chapter 11" in print or else I was some sort of liar. Maybe I wasn't comfortable showing that thorn yet. I felt a lot of shame about going bankrupt. It was a hard story to tell and it still is. But there I was, trying to write a book that motivates people and guides them to make better decisions with their lives, and the only thing that guy cared about was that *one* detail. More than a million people file for bankruptcy every year, and that's a beautiful thing about America—you get second chances.

If you follow me on social media, you know how spiteful some people can be. I'm exposed on a global scale, so I get it from all over. It's par for the course when the public has access to your life. If you're a local business owner, you'll hear competitors talking behind your back, disgruntled former employees will write anonymous negative reviews or comments on the Internet, and others who are just jealous of your success will attempt to sabotage you. I've gotten used to it. Like Gandhi said, "First they ignore you. Then they laugh at you. Then they fight you. Then you win."

It's Okay to Care

One time in a meeting, my boss at the time, Keith Howington, the CEO of Logix, said, "Ryan cares a lot about what people think." It was true, but I didn't like it. I was the youngest VP in the room, and it made me extremely self-conscious. For all I knew, I was going to be in engineering for the rest of my life. I cared so much about how others saw me that I made sure I was the best at communicating and the most efficient at my job, and I constantly overachieved to the point where people probably hated me. I really cared.

I still care about what people think, that never went away, but I've come to terms with it. If I really want to know what my fan base thinks of me, for instance, I just have to look at my social media accounts. But the only ones whose opinions actually matter are my family, my son, my closest friends, and my team members. Now, when I get a compliment from one of them, I accept it, and feel appreciation.

It's okay to care about pleasing others, gaining their approval, and getting affirmation—only choose carefully. Otherwise you'll waste your life trying to win the favor of people who will never ever approve of you.

Likewise, you should appreciate the success of others. When I hear someone is doing well, or if I see my neighbor just added an addition to his house or bought a new car, I don't question how he or she was able to afford something. Instead I say, "Congratulations." And I think, *Well, that person must be doing something right. I'll ask for a meeting.* As Jay Z said, "Every day a star is born—clap for 'em." If there's an artist who intrigues me, I'll invite him over. I don't say, "Well, you know, he just got lucky, because Andy Warhol mentored him." Instead, I say I'd love to meet the guy and learn about his art. I try not to shut myself off from opportunities by being caught up in judging others. I always want to stay open and learn, so if someone can teach me how they did what they did, then I'm all ears.

The lessons here are: Own your image, take into account that the public's view of you will be colored by their perceptions, and it's okay to care what people think, but don't let lesser people get to you. And when all that fails, try making your haters a playlist. Mine starts with Nas's "Hate Me Now," then "Hate" by Jay Z, "Paparazzi" by Xzibit, "I Made It" by Cash Money Heroes, and "No Love" by Eminem. It's great motivation in the gym.

Love Thy Neighbor

One of my friends, Robert Stevanovski, chairman of ACN, recently reminded me of a quote: "The best way to beat an enemy is to make them your friend."

Shortly after the police incident I was summoned to a meeting by the city attorney and various other law enforcement officials to discuss the noise and light violations with my neighbors. Unfortunately, my house is made of glass and steel and is situated on top of a hill; basically it's right on top of my neighbor's home. His complaint was that even the mildest noises sound like they're being blasted via megaphone into his house. This was serious; there were big fines and penalties for me if we couldn't find solutions to these problems.

My attorney advised me on a strategy for the meeting, but I already knew what I was going to do—I was going to reinvent this antagonistic relationship, and take my neighbor from enemy to friend.

If you haven't noticed, this is the exact opposite of my nature and my temper, but I knew it was the right thing to do. So, I walked into the meeting with my two lawyers, prepared to defend my rights as a homeowner, but also to listen to my neighbor's concerns and seek solutions and compromises. The look of shock on their faces was priceless. They had assumed I'd send my attorneys to the meeting for me, and they were surprised I was there. I got credit just for showing up; it meant I cared.

After about a hundred apologies (the minimum number my

lawyer instructed me to make) and coming up with various solutions—possibly a line of trees or other sound-buffering elements that we could put in place—by the end of it, I became friends with my sole antagonist.

I got his e-mail address through his attorney and I looked him up. It turns out he's a writer like me, only I write early in the morning and he writes at night. As an author I can identify. This is a guy whose writing is being interrupted, and there should be mutual respect between us, even if we don't share a passion for words.

After that meeting I realized this man was just seeking the right to write, and the last thing I wanted to do was damage a person's artistic work. Now we send e-mails back and forth to each other, and we may not be playing the same "music," at the same times, but my neighbor is a rock star artist, and rock stars should have mutual respect.

CHAPTER 15

WHAT WEAKENS YOU STRENGTHENS YOU

This story doesn't end with me walking off into the sunset, but it does end with me in a wheelchair.

I was celebrating with my Kabbalah family one night on a recent trip to Israel. We were going around the table discussing what we would like to do that we hadn't already done on this very personal and spiritual journey. When the question came around to me, I said that I wanted to play basketball again, as I hadn't in years. Specifically, I wanted to dunk again. If you've ever dunked a basketball, you know exactly the feeling I'm referring to. It's the closest thing to flying that I can think of.

I'm a morning person and I don't sleep much. As soon as I open my eyes, I'm so excited by life, I jump out of bed and get to work, or work out, or do both. This morning was no exception. Waking up in my hotel room in Israel at 5 a.m., I went straight to my balcony to view the sunrise. The beauty of this foreign land is something almost holy to me (it's called the Holy Land for a reason)—and what did I see in the light of the rising sun? A basketball court.

With a boyish smile on my face I rushed downstairs to the court and started playing. Soon my travel mates, hearing the patter of the ball hitting pavement, would join me as I worked five years of rust off my game. I was working up a good sweat in the morning sun, and encouraged by some positive feedback from my "audience," I decided to go in for a dunk.

As my feet lifted off the court, one of my kneecaps also lifted—it completely tore from its attachment and lodged up inside the front of my thigh. When I landed, the rest of my knee blew out—tendons, ligaments, meniscus, everything. I stayed in the exact spot where I came down, awaiting my fate for several hours.

As the owner of a health and weight-loss company, I can tell you that I haven't always lived the healthiest life possible. In my youth, I abused my body with excess, and this was one of the consequences. I'm thirty-nine years old. I don't have much fear in me, and I rarely listen to my body, even when I'm in pain. Most of my scars are from old fistfights I got into as a kid, and from other accidents as a result of my misguided youth.

They scooped me up off the basketball court and loaded me onto a gurney and drove me to a hospital in a rural town in Israel, escorted by an elite Navy SEAL assigned to protect me on this trip. I lay there, typing out this story on my iPhone, smiling through the pain. I got the message from my body loud and clear.

I often use sports analogies when I'm writing, and my favorite sport is basketball. I don't believe in coincidences. When you study Kabbalah, you learn rapidly and you attempt to connect with the spirit and energy of the miracle makers of our time. Jesus was a Kabbalist, and I was praying to him to heal me. I had never taken a vacation for spiritual reasons before. I was in a place where I was rapidly transforming—this year had been difficult professionally and personally, and to add insult to injury, now physically, too.

I lay there wondering if my trip was over. I felt bad that I had taken all the fun from my travel companions and pointed all this energy toward myself. Would I need extensive surgery? How long would it take to heal? Would I ever jump again? Dunk a basketball again?

My injury showed me how easy it is to take things for granted. My flight out of Israel couldn't have been any more different than it was from when we arrived. I sat there in a wheelchair, my injured leg straight out with the other leg under it for support, being wheeled through the most secure airport in the world. The expression on my face spoke the thousand or so words that my pride couldn't. I could no longer walk into the room like a rock star; for the next four months I would be learning to walk again.

My number one counterintuitive philosophy is, "What weakens you, strengthens you."

To build a muscle, first you have to break it down. To heal a wound, your body makes scar tissue. When you experience pain, your tolerance for pain goes up. When you suffer, you strengthen.

In fact, the fastest way to grow is to suffer. Whether self-imposed or delivered by the hand of God, in the moments when I am at my worst, I realize I am also at my best.

The year 2015 was one of the most challenging years for me, and also the most rewarding. I started out with the best of intentions, but in February I learned that my company's head of security was being charged with numerous felonies. My life was turned upside down once again.

Suffering is the greatest teacher. Responding to events I didn't plan for, experiencing the biggest injury of my life, and still having to work and fight during that time—it made me strong. I had many moments of weakness, and rock-bottom moments, over those twelve months, but I reached inside and found the strength to keep going. What I took away from this is that you can only learn who you are when you question who you are, and you only really question yourself when you are weak. You could say that 2015 was the year I got to know myself better than ever before, and self discovery is a fucking chore.

I study the lives of great entrepreneurs so that I can learn from them. One of the greatest examples is the late Steve Jobs. He needed to be weak before he could be strong, he needed to be humiliated to grow his resolve, and he needed to be humbled to go back to Apple after being forced out. I thought about this a lot in 2015, as I worked to reinvent the company I bought back a little over a year ago. Some days I schedule sixteen-plus hours of meetings, putting together plans for the coming year and developing the tactics necessary to achieve the strategy. In 2016, heading into the launch of this book, and the start of what I plan to be my best year yet, I'm stronger than I've ever been because I've been weaker than I've ever been.

I've also learned that, vice versa, what makes you strong will one day make you weak.

Shortly after I injured myself in Israel, I had to give a speech in Cancun. They wheeled me into the room in a wheelchair, and I delivered my speech with my foot propped up on a couch. My topic that day was strengths and weaknesses. At ViSalus we're so obsessed with strengths that we tested hundreds of our team members so that we can understand everyone's strengths and weaknesses. One of the people I hired to help us graph these strengths and look for holes in our company was the maker of StrengthsFinder.com, Clifton StrengthsFinder, and one of their consultants had flown out to Cancun to help educate us on our individual strengths and work with us as a team.

According to Clifton StrengthsFinder, there are no weaknesses. There are only strengths, because in every strength is an implicit weakness. The way they describe it is that each strength has a basement, the dark side of your strength, and a balcony, when that strength is operating in a good way.

For instance, in my list of top five strengths is "competition," and used to describe the balcony of competition with words and phrases like: driven, motivated, wanting to be number one, measurement oriented, and "you're a winner." The basement of competition is: sore loser, not a team player, puts down others, self-centered, and confrontational. The following story is about me being in the basement with my number one strength, you guessed it: competition.

For the first five years of ViSalus, when we were the underdogs, I often asked myself, *Why the hell am I in the direct-selling industry. It's one of the most competitive industries out there.* And the competition is unscrupulous. They attack, fabricate lies, and bash each other like politicians on the campaign trail. In our industry, we have that times ten. And we're not just competing with companies in our industry, it comes from outside the industry as well; Apple, Amazon, and Uber are all coming up with direct-to-consumer health solutions.

One day I was handed a copy of a contract from one of my competitors. It had been sent to me by one of my team members they had been trying to recruit. My team member, one of my most loyal who had been with us since we started the business, had engaged in lengthy discussions with the competition about leaving ViSalus, so as to gain competitive intel. Essentially, he was a mole. What we learned was that because of our extreme competitiveness—being a sore loser, putting down others, and being confrontational—our competition felt that they had no choice but to unionize. We had alienated so many of our competitors that they had all turned against us. Competition is always against you, but now they had teamed up.

Not only were they unionized, but there was a mandate in the contract that specified if this team member were to leave ViSalus, and the deal didn't work out, they were free to join any other company—except ViSalus.

I remember thinking to myself, *Why the hell would they bribe and steal a team member from me, and then if it doesn't work out, prohibit them from coming back to me, even if they wanted to?*

Their strategy was simple. They didn't care whether it worked out or not; they were willing to pay millions of dollars just to take an asset away from us. And it wasn't just that one competitor; all of them had drawn up the same contract because they all had one common enemy: us.

My strategy of beating the competition fair and square, one by one, had worked marvelously until now—but we couldn't compete against all of them all at once. I was completely blindsided. It never dawned on me that competitors would gang up like that. There are highly intelligent people in my industry, and the reason we've chosen this industry is because we know we can make hundreds of millions, if not billions, of dollars here. Some of the most formidable competitors had now started attacking us and our products, day in and day out, and their strategy was starting to work. I lost some of my very best people. It was terrible.

At first I was upset about it. But you can only be a sore loser if you occasionally win, and I hadn't had a win in months. If you don't win sometimes, you're not a sore loser, you're just a loser. Having completely missed seeing this competitive strategy against us made me realize that we had been operating almost entirely in the basement. We can't be confrontational with competition constantly, otherwise that energy would get returned to us. We had to make the intellectual adjustment, and go from thinking, *We're better than them* to *We're better than this*. Get out of the basement and onto the balcony.

I never understood that competition had such an ugly basement. But it does. When you're in the trenches of corporate battle, a lot of times you're operating out of fear. And fear is what plunges us into the dark side of our strengths. And sometimes our greatest strength can be our greatest weakness. So, think about this as you pause to strategize about the future. We shouldn't fear death; death is easy. It's life that's complicated. The human body and spirit were made to take a beating, but everything that doesn't kill you *doesn't* make you stronger—it's what *weakens* you that strengthens you.

CHAPTER 16
SURVIVAL SKILLS

n March 2011, after my stepdad passed away, I decided to take some time off and travel. I knew ViSalus was going to have a big year; we had already made $231 million in sales. I was just finishing up the manuscript of *Nothing to Lose,* and I decided to add an epilogue reflecting on my stepfather Bob's death before sending it to the editor one final time.

While Bob was still breathing, but had in effect lost his life, I watched all the people who were soon to inherit his money come visit him and pay him their last respects. My stepfather was notoriously tight. The irony was that he had never even flown first class, and now these people would be taking first-class flights to his funeral on his dime. There's nothing like the death of a parent to remind you of your mortality. I thought, *Fuck, I don't want to die like that. I want to enjoy life now.*

I hate to call it a "bucket list," so I decided to build a "fuck it" list. I thought about where I wanted to be in that moment, and right at the top of the list was Carnival in Brazil. The opulence and extravagance of an exotic culture, a world away from Los Angeles, was exactly the type of vacation I had dreamed I'd someday have enough money to experience. It was a total fantasy. I was newly single. I decided to live my life.

One of the people I invited to go with me was my friend Matt Sinerich; the trip was a birthday gift to him for helping me reboot ViSalus. I bought our plane tickets and rented a ten thousand square foot house in Florianópolis. The first night we got there, we asked our driver where to go out, and it turned out that the place we had rented was forty minutes away from all the popular night clubs. So, we headed down to the Floripa club scene in our party bus and were met with a spectacle I had only seen on TV and had been dreaming about ever since I was a young man: tens of thousands of people, women dancing in the streets, the best music in the world, and a culture of pure celebration. We dove in head first. I had no access, so I had to bribe my way into the clubs. I bought a $10,000 table, and committed to at least another $10,000 in alcohol. We weren't going to spare any expense to have the best experience possible.

We came tumbling out of the club at 11 a.m. the next day, dripping sweat from dancing and squinting in the sunlight, which we hadn't seen for hours. The parking lot was nearly empty—we were literally the last people standing—except for what looked like a group of characters harassing my driver. My first thought was, *Is this safe?* Brazil is known to have kidnappers. As I got closer I saw a tall dark-haired man waving a wad of cash at my driver, and my driver shaking his head no. There were two other men in the group, and I could hear them speaking English. Satisfied that they weren't Brazilian kidnappers, I walked up. They looked as dumbfounded as I was—I guess they weren't used to being told no when they had a handful of cash.

We were far from town, and there were no cabs. Luckily, my driver was loyal and was stalling them; he explained they were being very insistent. At first I thought, *No fucking way.* I was tired, and I had every excuse not to say yes. But then another voice told me, *Let's see where this goes.*

I said, "Do you need a ride?" They said yes, but it turned out that their home was forty-five minutes in the opposite direction to mine. Something inside me said, *Fuck it. Give these guys a ride.*

The dark-haired man turned out to be Sam Ben-avraham, an influential men's fashion entrepreneur. When he got into the car, he looked at me and said, "You just changed your life," with a huge smile on his face.

We ended up hanging out for three days during Carnival, where Sam repaid me by graciously waving me into impossible-to-get into events. I no longer had to bribe my way into clubs for the rest of the trip. On day three of nonstop Carnival partying, Sam and I somehow wound up on the beach, still going after a long night. Neither of us had any doubt about the other being successful, but at this point we hadn't talked about what we did for a living. Our bond was simple. I had done him a favor and he reciprocated it, and we were both having the time of our lives. But we started to talk about work a little, so I mentioned that I was writing a book and told him the title. At first he kind of dismissed it—a lot of people say they're writing a book—and then out of politeness he asked, "What's the title?"

I said, "*Nothing to Lose, Everything to Gain.*"

Sam's face brightened, "That's a great title. It's going to be a hit."

When I saw Sam's spontaneous reaction, I thought, *This is a guy who knows brands, and knows what people want. If he thinks it's going to be a massive success, I must have something special.*

I had gotten a lot of shit from Blyth for writing the book. The feeling I got was that the bigger I built my brand, the less control they felt they had over me. Or maybe they were scared I would make them look bad, or embarrass them. Even my partners, Nick and Blake, who were totally behind it, wanted to read the book first before they would support it. As a result, I had lots of doubts.

After Sam said it was going to be a hit, it gave me the encouragement I needed, and I returned home from my trip more confident than ever to finish the book.

As I left for Rio and we parted ways, Sam invited me to his home in Miami for his party at the Ultra Music Festival a few weeks later. I'm socially awkward, so my first inclination is to say no to everything. (I'm the type of guy who gets a wedding invitation and replies with: Sorry can't make it, maybe next time.) But I knew, based on firsthand experience of seeing Sam party in Brazil, it was going to be out of control, and I couldn't miss his event. I said yes.

A few weeks later, I walked into Sam's mansion in Miami

and was greeted by the sounds of will.i.am and Puff Daddy performing inside. There were no more than a hundred people at the event, but among them were famous DJs, musicians, fashion icons, and some of the most beautiful models in the world. I noticed in Sam's collection of artwork were stunning photographs with what looked like strange, Mad Max–looking people in the desert. He told me he had taken the photographs himself.

Over the next few days we went to the Ultra Music Festival to immerse ourselves, and then returned to Sam's house to sit at the twenty-foot-long outdoor dining table to enjoy course after course. By day four, we had eaten all the lobster in Miami and danced the last pieces of ourselves into the ground. We decided to go out for a Brazilian dinner. Thirty of us gathered together, feeling oddly energized even though we were exhausted. I sat there at that table that night in awe that a simple, unselfish decision had led me to this wonderful place among new friends. It's almost as though God had given me a last supper. As I was gorging myself on Brazilian food that night, back in LA, my mother was walking up the stairs in her home to go to bed, with her cell phone in one hand and a glass of wine in the other. The reason I know this is because the next day they found her lying in a pool of blood at the base of the marble stairs with her skull cracked open, shattered glass everywhere, and her cell phone had frozen on the exact time she had fallen.

When I left Miami, I landed in Michigan, checked my phone, and found a text from my brother-in-law, the police chief. It read: "Your mother is in the hospital. It doesn't look like she's going to make it. She has fallen down a flight of stairs. Call me back."

I canceled my meeting and walked up to the ticket counter and said, "I need to get back to Los Angeles immediately."

It was March 29, 2011. There was a flight leaving for LA in forty-five minutes and they put me on it. While I sat at the gate waiting for my flight, I turned off my phone. I didn't want an update. I didn't want to know if she was dead or not. I couldn't spend four and a half hours on a flight knowing my mother was dead. I wanted hope.

Two hours into the flight, I pulled out my laptop. I had spent the entire time praying, and I had the idea that I should get some other people to pray for my mother. I got onto Facebook, where I had a few thousand followers. I thought, *I'm going to let my friends know I need their help.*

I posted: My mother has fallen down a flight of stairs. Please pray for her.

I kept praying, *Please, God, let me see my mother again.* I didn't know why, but it felt like it was the only way I could get through the flight. I had never felt more alone in my life, and I fly alone all the time. No one could experience what I was going through but me.

The last time I had seen my mother was on St. Patrick's Day, March 17, before I left for Brazil. My sister Stephanie had invited everyone over to her house for a traditional Irish dinner. My mother was in bad shape. We were all grieving the loss of Bob, but she was really taking it hard. She had started hitting the bottle again, and taking all sorts of prescription pills. She was so weak that when we pulled up to the house, she got out of the car and started to tumble backward. I had to rush over to catch her.

It was an omen of what was to come. I thought, *If she can't even get out of the car, she's going to hurt herself.* I knew she was going to fall eventually, but it just didn't occur to me to take it as seriously as I should have.

We had already had a family intervention with her, but it only made her sneakier. Stephanie went and checked on her every day, and my mom would wait until after she left so she could drink without guilt. It reminded me of when I was a kid and she'd secretly drink; we'd come home from school and find her passed out with bottles stashed all over the house. She was so helpless . . . and so were we.

When I landed in Los Angeles, I drove immediately to the hospital to see her. I disobeyed every traffic law known to mankind, and it wasn't long before I saw flashing lights in my rearview mirror and pulled over. The officer came up with his hand on his gun (it must have looked like I was fleeing a bank robbery), and when I rolled down my tinted windows, he took one look at my face and asked me what was wrong.

I said, "I'm on my way to the hospital. I think my mom is dead. I have no idea where it is." The officer looked at me with sympathy, ran back to his car, pulled in front of me, and escorted me to the UCLA Medical Center several miles away.

I walked into the hospital and saw my aunt, my sister, and my cousins standing there in the lobby. By the looks on their faces, the situation didn't seem as bad as I had been led to believe. My mother had been in brain surgery for eight hours, with no updates. I didn't have accurate information, and neither did they. They had been calmly waiting.

Finally, a surgeon came out. I stood up and walked over to him, and let him know that his patient was my mother.

He said, "We've done all that we can. It is very bad."

"Is she going to make it?" I asked.

I could tell he chose his words carefully. "I can tell you that less than two percent of people in her condition make it," he said.

Nothing could have prepared me for what I saw when I walked into my mother's hospital room. I could barely recognize her: her eyes were black-and-blue, her head was completely shaved, her teeth were knocked out, and half of her skull had been removed for the operation. It was a gruesome sight; she had a mass of tubes and suction cups coming in and out of her brain. I never realized how beautiful my mother really was until I saw her like this.

I went over to the side of the bed and gently picked up her hand. I said, "Mom, do you know who I am?" She squeezed my hand, and I could hear her softly mumbling my name. She knew who I was. I felt a flood of gratitude in my heart. But the moment of awareness wouldn't last. Later that night she had an extreme seizure that ripped through her brain like an aftershock and sent her into a deep coma. We didn't know whether she would wake up or not.

The doctor came out to ask me if we should resuscitate her should she begin to go back into a coma. I was completely in the dark, but I had just felt her squeeze my hand earlier, and so I said, "Yes. We will resuscitate."

He just stared at me, with unsaid words behind his eyes. Like he thought I was making the wrong decision.

Mercy or a Miracle

On August 4, 2011, my book dropped. It rose rapidly up the *New York Times* best-seller list, debuting at number three. I was ecstatic. Just after I had gotten the news about my book, I received a phone call from Kasie, my son's mom. I had been very concerned about Reagan; he wasn't acting like normal kids act. I thought maybe it was his hearing, so we took him in to get tested. It turned out that he had autism. By some bizarre twist of fate, I would learn of his diagnosis on the same day my book dropped. Also, that same day I was informed that I received legal custodianship of my mother, so that we could eventually make the decision legally to take her off life support.

I regretted saying yes to resuscitating my mother. She remained in the deep, dark hole she had fallen into. I was visiting her almost every day I was in Los Angeles, but not as often as I wanted to because I knew she'd be upset with me if I let her accident stop me from becoming a success. I was on the road for press and for ViSalus events and I was doing all this because I was inspired by her.

My friend Sam had seen my Facebook post asking for prayers. To my surprise, he reached out to me with more sympathy and concern than I would have expected from a new friend. In one of our conversations, I explained to him what I was going through with my mother and he told me, "You need to come to Burning Man. You need this." Knowing my tendency to cancel everything, he went out of his way to make sure I'd go; he paid for everything, he arranged everything, and he gave me no excuse not to go.

Right before I took off for Burning Man, I went to a tattoo artist and had "8-4-11" tattooed on my forearm in black ink to mark the tragedy of life, the day that God had challenged me the hardest. A week later I went out to Black Rock City to join Sam. I remember that the scab on my tattoo, after just a week, was infected. I felt I was carrying around a lifetime of grief and guilt, and now I had an irritated, red, visible reminder of it.

I allowed Sam to plan everything. I was going out to the desert to surrender my ego, my control, and my beliefs about what I thought I knew about life. I wanted to do some deep soul-searching and get lost in the desert with people I didn't know.

I wandered for days through all kinds of campgrounds and different groups of people. I hoped to take some of Burning Man's artistic inspiration back with me to apply it to my company. I liked the ingenuity I saw, and being in a society with a different set of rules, rules not based on commercialism or capitalism. When I was hungry, I was surprised to find that someone would feed me. There's no commerce there, so you can't buy food or a bottle of water, but you can give and be given to. On the last night of Burning Man, the participants burn all the structures, leaving the *playa* just as they found it, with no litter or trash. It's a test of a different way of life and society.

On one of the afternoons that I was walking around getting lost, I came upon a structure about 500,000 square feet in diameter, a sculpture made of wood called the Temple. People would go there to pray and meditate, even get married. On the outside of the edifice, people had inscribed names and written about things they wanted to leave behind after their experience at Burning Man. I read messages: someone asking forgiveness, or missing a dead relative or a lost child, or saying they were sorry that they didn't say good-bye to their mother. I could feel the energy of the thousands of pen passages and inscriptions, and I took out my pen to write my own.

Dear Mom. I'm sorry you fell. I wish I could have caught you. I love you. I'm sorry I never told you how much I loved you. I pray you'll have either mercy or a miracle.

Then I signed it, just like I signed every birthday card, every Christmas card, every Mother's Day card I had ever given my mother.

I love you,
Ryan.

I asked for mercy first because every day I begged God that I would get the telephone call telling me that my mother had passed away, and I wouldn't have to take her off life support myself. In reality I never really believed I could receive a miracle, but of course, some part of me wished that she would just wake up.

The last day of the trip, I sat in silence and watched the Temple burn. My ink was now mixed with the dirt and ashes of our deepest hopes, feelings, and regrets. I had gone to Burning Man hoping to find mercy or a miracle, and even though I didn't know it, I had planted the seeds for both.

Why I'm Here

I was standing on stage at the AmericanAirlines Arena in Miami. Every seat was sold out; I was looking out over a sea of more than eighteen thousand people. I squinted my eyes and saw people sitting in the very back of the arena, and thought, *Fuck. They can't see me. They can't even hear me. How am I going to offer them anything of value?*

I took a moment backstage alone and dropped to my knees and started to pray, "Our Father who art in heaven . . ." I asked God to help me deliver His message and not mine. To be a messenger. To help me resist my ego and find the true talents granted to me, and the energy to connect deeply with the person in the arena who needed it the most. To lead these people from negative to positive.

As I stepped out onto that stage, I heard a roar of applause. I thought, *If only they knew what I was going through.*

Back in California, my mother was still in a coma, lying in a hospital bed on life support. She had been in a vegetative state for almost sixteen months. We were losing hope. I knew what had to be done, and yet I wasn't sure I could do it. A few months after our Miami event, I sat down and wrote my three-year-old son Reagan a letter:

> Dear Reagan,
>
> I am writing you because I want you to learn from what I've learned.
>
> Right now we are finalizing your grandma's (my mom's) end of life. She's on life support and it's been 18 months. She always told me that she didn't want to be a "vegetable" and unfortunately, because she didn't have a living will, she is just what she didn't want to be.
>
> I hope you'll have the strength to honor my wishes and take me off life support should I ever become a vegetable, or ask you to do so.
>
> I love you, son. This is very hard for me; you don't know this now but you give me the strength to be a good father to you while I grieve as a son. I love you always.
>
> Ryan—Dad

There's no book you can read or seminar you can take for how to be strong, there are only those who model it for you. In that moment, without knowing it, that's exactly what I was modeling—strength.

The next big speech was just a few months away, on November 4, 2012. Now we were only one week away from pulling the plug. After battling for nearly two years, we had finally made the decision. I never missed a national ViSalus event before. As the day drew nearer, I thought, *Should I cancel? Should I spend every last minute of my mom's life with her? Or should I be a leader and show strength?* I would pray ten times a day, and still the question remained unanswered.

This decision was one of the hardest I've ever been faced with. *Do I go speak to my team, or do I sit next to my mother's bedside?* I felt weak. There just didn't seem to be an answer. Finally, I changed the question. I thought, *Would my mom want to see her only son fail as a leader because of her?* With that question, there was no question at all. I knew the answer: I had to go speak. I felt my strength return renewed. I had to show everyone in that stadium that no matter what you're going through, you *can* get through it.

I got on Facebook and posted: I only have a few days left with my mother before she passes away and I'm coming to this event; WHAT'S YOUR EXCUSE?

I felt so clear about my decision, I thought it would be received with the same intention with which it was created. It was not.

The uproar was overwhelming. People were threatening to boycott the event. One of my sales leaders called me and said, "Ryan, hundreds of people are going to walk out of the room when you take the stage." Seeing all the negative comments, I broke down in tears. My heart was broken. I was trying to do what my mother would have wanted, so that I could honor her wishes in her absence, and all I got back was hatred.

My resolve weakened, and after going back and forth on it

for hours, I almost caved in. I consulted my cofounders and asked, "Should I attend?" They said, "Yes. We've got your back."

I flew to St. Louis less than ten days before my mother would die. I had an image in my head of a ten-thousand-person exodus, and I couldn't shake it. I was afraid of being rejected. One of the only things that gave me the resolve to walk onto that stage was that I knew there was somebody in that audience who was going through a difficult time, like I was, and they could use my strength as an anchor to windward. I took a deep breath, silently asked God to support me in the decision I had made, and stepped onto the stage.

My speech was simple. It was titled: "Why I Am Here."

I addressed the audience. My voice was heavy, monotone, and exhausted. "As some of you know, my family is nearing the end of an eighteen-month journey; over that eighteen months I've had one family to turn to—ViSalus. Loyalty is the thing I value the most. It's the way I was raised: that when times are tough, loyalty is all you can count on."

I paused; the room was completely silent. Then someone screamed out, "We love you, Ryan." It was a woman's voice. When I heard that, I smiled, and the audience went crazy. They rose to their feet and gave me a standing ovation. I had to hold back the tears. The message had finally gotten across.

Everyone goes through hardships and gets hit with trage-dies. I believe that as leaders, we should be an example to others. So many people on social media hadn't understood my decision, or my explanation of it. However, I don't want to be the kind of leader business schools and consulting firms pump out, pretending to know all the answers. I may have superpowers, but I'm not superhuman. Pretending I'm not living in the same world as others doesn't help me lead them. Something in my gut told me I had to do this, so I did. My company needed me and, it turns out, my mother needed those ten thousand prayers.

Being a leader can be lonely, and to have such a wonderful show of support gave me the strength to make the next difficult decision.

Blink Once

I felt responsible for taking my mother off life support, but thank God my sisters, my aunt Sandy, and the rest of the family supported me. My mother had left no living will, so we had to get affidavits from friends and relatives to get the court to rule on whether or not we would be allowed to take her off life support. It was a long process; by the time we were done, we had sent twenty-five letters to the court.

We finally received the court order approving our request for removal of life support. In my mother's case, removing her from life support meant they'd remove her feeding tube, her breathing tube, and they'd stop vacuuming out her lungs. Every day while she had been in a coma, she had her lungs cleared of liquid— almost two liters of fluids—three to five times a day. When I started to do the math to figure out how long it would take my mother to die when life support was removed, I realized, to my

horror, that she wouldn't be leaving this existence peacefully—
she'd die of drowning.

I knew my mom. My mother wouldn't have wanted to die a
"natural" slow death, convulsing, covered in slime, and choking
on her own vomit—she would have wanted to leave pumped full
of morphine, with a smile on her face. I started frantically calling around to every care facility in the state. It took a few days to
find the right hospice to take her; they agreed to heavily sedate
her during the process so that she wouldn't feel her lungs filling
up with fluid. I went to the hospital the next day to see my mother
and to tell her that she wouldn't be in pain when we ended her
life. It was the least we could do.

My sister and aunt were just leaving when I arrived at the
building; I saw them briefly in the parking lot. One of my security team who had been a medic came with me; he had been a
big help during the entire process. I walked into my mother's
room and looked at her. We made eye contact, her eyes dilated,
and she focused on me.

I froze.

For two years I had been experiencing these false positives—
moments when I swore my mother was looking at me, and then
her eyes would drift to another spot. Her eyes jumped all over
the room; she couldn't connect with anything she was seeing,
she couldn't focus, and she definitely didn't recognize me.

Something was different this time. I leaned down next to
her. I said, "Blink once for yes, or twice for no. Mom, do you know
who I am?"

She blinked once.

Was it possible? I asked her two more times, and both times she answered yes. With tears in my eyes, I put my arm around her neck and laid my head down on her chest (the only way you can safely hug someone with a skull fracture). My ear was very close to her tracheotomy tube, and I heard the faintest whisper coming from her throat. I heard her say, "Ryan."

I jumped up and immediately called my sister. "She's up," I said. "Mom's up. She said my name."

There was hesitation on the other end. "Ryan, I know it's going to be hard on you to end Mom's life," Stephanie said. "She's not up. She's been doing this for two years."

"She's up," I said. But I remember thinking to myself, *Am I crazy?*

Then Stephanie handed the phone to my aunt Sandy. I could hear the notes of sympathy and exhaustion in her voice. "Ryan, I know this is tough on you—"

"Fuck you guys, *she's up!*" I said. "We're not ending her life tomorrow."

I had never screamed at my sister or my aunt before. I was so mad.

The next day my sister and her husband went to see Mom in the hospital. I rushed over, so I would be there when they were there, and they could see what I had seen. They had gotten there before me, and when I walked into the room, they were sitting there by my mother's bed, laughing with her! In twenty-four hours, my mother had somehow gone from making basic eye contact to laughing, mimicking us, and squeezing our hands.

My sister just looked at me and said, "She's up."

My mother's health continued to improve, and by February 2013, my miracle mom had her first meal in two years. I flew in from my paperback-book tour to share a Thanksgiving-style feast with her. I had been skipping holiday dinners for two years; I felt guilty eating a big meal with the family when my mother was lying in bed with a feeding tube in her throat.

The date that I have inscribed on my arm—8-4-11—means something different to me now. I used to say it was one dose of pleasure and two doses of pain. It meant that God was challenging me, but it also meant that I would have given anything to have traded that one dose of pleasure—hitting the *New York Times* best-seller list—for my mother's and my son's health. For two years, the tattoo meant what I would have sacrificed for the love of my family. Now the tattoo has a positive meaning. If it weren't for the amazing duality of this milestone, I would have had it removed. Now it's there to remind me that it won't be the last time I have to deal with difficulty and tragedy. Life will be filled with those. But now the tattoo has a symbolic meaning: that if you hold on to what you know to be true, you can get through anything.

Beautiful Pain

I was in Detroit at my company's 2016 launch event, feeling high off the hard work that we had put in to our collective ambitions. I was sitting in a booth that must have been built in the '70s in a dimly lit bar at the DoubleTree in Detroit, talking with one of my top company leaders, Jason O'Toole, when I received a simple text from my sister Stephanie.

"Hey, Ry, our cousin Randy passed away."

Jason saw me grab my phone for a quick text check and then probably the next thing he saw was my heart, on my sleeve. I rarely make calls in the company of others, or abruptly remove myself from a conversation, but, in shock, I immediately called Steph back. I went from being strong in "business mode" to feeling weak with regret; Randy was like a brother to me—we grew up together. I was sorry that I hadn't engaged with him the way he had with me. Then it hit me, with grief, that his mother—my aunt Tonnie—had just lost her son. And worse, he had a six-month-old son.

The last time we had connected was when my grandmother Winni passed away. He shared with me that I was an inspiration to him and that he wanted to connect at a deeper level. And there I was, one hour after receiving the news of his death, standing in the flames of a beautiful pain. With remorse, sadness, a feeling of helplessness, and holding back tears—because my aunt Tonnie didn't need to hear another voice of sorrow—I sent her a simple message: "What can I do to help?"

I regret not being able to fulfill his wishes and connect with him like I should have, but I felt a weight lift from my spirit when I sent those words. It was like he was sitting in the room with me, looking down with a smile on his face.

I'm sharing this story with you because this is the epitome of my life story. For every high point in my life, every time I soar, I am immediately brought down to Earth by a tragedy. My life is a series of 8-4-11s. If I am a soldier for God, then I am well battle tested. I can only guess why He chooses to test me in this way, but I do know that with every beautiful pain I receive, in that flame, I find the light.

Compartmentalize and Survive

Isolating and focusing separately on difficult issues is something I've done my entire life, probably as a result of my upbringing and the early trauma I experienced. I first noticed the effects of compartmentalization in business in 2012, when I found myself juggling a rocky IPO process, fighting the courts to take my mother off life support, changing my entire company's culture, and struggling to make progress with my son's autism. I had a very successful year despite the private and professional roller coaster. I had to accept the fact that I could only do so much. I had many areas that required my focus, but only a limited amount of emotional and mental energy to devote to any of them.

Normally, entrepreneurs think about their businesses all day long. In the past I would have worked on a long list of projects. Instead, I had so much demanding attention from both my mind and my heart that I had to prioritize, and focus on only the few things that mattered the most.

I developed a system. Every time I was hit with a new crisis or an extreme challenge I would compartmentalize it, isolate it from all the other challenges. Then, when I was ready, I would apply extreme focus on one compartment, but only for a short period of time. Once I saw some incremental progress, I would then close that compartment and open the next one. Anything that didn't deserve a compartment, I would say no to.

As an entrepreneur, you're going to get hit by big, traumatic, potentially harmful, or life-changing events, sometimes in succession—the stress of being a father or mother, potentially running out of capital, being rejected by an investor (or several investors), getting slapped with lawsuits, or suddenly losing the public's favorable opinion of you or your company. The only way you'll survive is if you learn how to compartmentalize your life.

It's very difficult to compartmentalize. Most people can't open up a compartment, make a little progress, and then close it. They're too emotionally attached to let go. These are the entrepreneurs that blow up their businesses when their marriages fail, or quit working when things don't go their way.

Here's a visual for compartmentalization. Pretend that something you're dealing with in your life is in a room where, when you walk in, you have to solve an equation on a whiteboard. There's a countdown clock showing less than an hour to get the problem solved, or take a single step in the right direction. Once you've done that, you shut the door and go into another room equally as important. Then you do this again, and again.

It sounds tiring, doesn't it? The alternative is much worse. If you're unable to isolate issues, and are letting traumatic life events affect your business, then you might not have a business for very long.

I've shared these experiences with you because survival has to be learned, and it isn't a lesson they teach you in business school.

CHAPTER 17
YOUR TURN

Recently, I was hanging out with one of my musician friends, a very talented vocalist, and I asked him, "What if all of a sudden you couldn't sing anymore?"

As a rock star singer he hadn't thought about that—he could hardly even fathom it.

Dumbfounded, he answered, "I'd commit suicide."

I said, "What if you kept your voice, but no one was ever allowed to hear it?"

He replied, "I'd commit suicide."

"So," I told him, "it isn't your voice that matters, it's the impact." As long as he's making that impact, he doesn't care how he does it.

"That's right," he said.

Just like my friend, the things that I do are a vehicle for me to make an impact. ViSalus, for instance, is highly optimized, and stylistically built around "the band" and my brand. Everything I do, including running ViSalus, is a vehicle designed for maximum impact. Me writing this book and you reading it brings me one step closer to fulfilling my purpose in life.

In *Nothing to Lose, Everything to Gain*, I talked about the importance of having a purpose statement, I even published mine in the book. In 2003, I said that it was my purpose to help people become independent from abuse and self-destruction, independent from confusion and economic burdens. I had to go through all of those first, so I could willingly share the lessons I learned with others, and they could do the same. I also wrote that I wanted to impact people—millions of people. At that time, I only impacted a hundred people, at best. So, millions of people was out of this world. But because I wrote down millions, somehow—consciously, subconsciously, and spiritually—I did it. Now the only adjustment I'd make to that purpose statement I wrote in 2003 is that my purpose is not to impact millions—but billions.

A lot of you might be reading this book right now and thinking, it can't be that simple. But it is. Trust me, every rock star who has walked out onto a stage was fulfilling their life's purpose. It's the struggle they faced, being on the road, the story they tell, and the difficulty they had in doing it—that's what makes them so great.

So, my final questions to you are: What is your purpose? What is your instrument? Who's in your band? And what rock-bottom moments will you be singing about?

ACKNOWLEDGMENTS

With much gratitude, I'd like to thank the many people in my life who supported me on this journey, whether I was at rock bottom or living my life like a rock star. First, thank you to my mother, Erla Hunt, for showing me with her incredible enduring strength how to be undefeatable in the face of impossible odds, and graceful even in adversity. Thank you to my son, Reagan, for inspiring me every day to be a better father, a better man, and a role model. Thank you Kasie Head for taking great care of my son and being a friend to me. And thank you to my sister Stephanie and her husband, Robert Gage, for being there for my mom when I could not. Thank you to my readers, and the millions of people who read *Nothing to Lose*, took a chance on me, my company, my ideas, on my strengths and my weaknesses. Thank you to God for answering my many whispered prayers, and for every second chance

You've given me. And thank you to my entire family, including those I call family but don't share blood with, because your love makes every failure and every victory worth it in the end.

There are several key people who helped make this book a reality who I would like to thank; my writing partner Shannon Constantine Logan for helping capture my voice since 2008; our editor Eric Nelson for enthusiastically pushing us forward; the highly skilled editorial team at Penguin Random House for polishing and publishing this book; and Carissa Bluestone for helping me "stick the landing." Thank you to the sales and marketing team at Penguin Random House, Tara Delaney Gilbride, Victoria Miller, Stefanie C. Rosenblum, and Kelsey Odorczyk, for giving this book a flawless launch. I'd like to thank my incredible literary agent, Kirby Kim of Janklow & Nesbit Associates, and his team, for believing in me and continuing to develop me as an author. A special thank you to my publicists Stephanie Jones and Stephanie Kahan at JONESWORKS Inc. for devoting their time and talent to this book launch, and Daniel Decker, for online marketing and promotional expertise. Thank you to Craig Clemons for being a sounding board. Thank you to Hasina Deary, director of my office, and right-hand (wo)man. Additionally, thank you to our project managers, assistants, and coordinators—Vivian Roberson at Portfolio and Brenna English-Loeb of Janklow—for keeping the book team connected and on schedule.

A big thank-you to photographers Quavondo Nguyen, Marvin Scott Jarrett, and Andrew Sandler for the book cover's photograph and promotional images, and Jaclynn Jarrett for producing, as well as their team members: Anthony Kimata, Melissa Lynn, Alan Fernandez, Bennet Perez, Dicko Chan, Natalie Fuller, Natalie Malchev, and Brittney Berault for assisting, photo-shoot lighting, makeup, and styling. Also, thank you to Chris Sergio, Karl Spurzman, and Tori Miller at Portfolio/Penguin for the final book cover design and publicity strategy and Bryan Stafford for working with me side by side for the past twenty years.

I work with many entrepreneurs, but these are some of the world's finest; a special thank-you to my brothers, Todd Goergen, Nick Sarnicola, Blake Mallen, Sam Ben-avraham, Matt Arnold, Matt Furey, Terrence Jenkins, Lewis Howes, Wilmer Valderrama, Jade Charles, Humble The Poet, Aldo Moreno, Jason Halpern, Rich Pala, the HashtagOne portfolio entrepreneurs I've invested in, and the Goergen family. Thank you to my teacher and mother Eliayu Jian.

Thank you to my ViSalus management team and our field leaders.

And most important, thank you for buying this book and sharing it. By doing so you have helped me fulfill my life's purpose. And together we will help countless people go from rock bottom to rock star.

CALL TO ACTION

Support the book!

Did you enjoy the book? Leave a review at: amazon.com, barnes andnoble.com, or goodreads.com. Or tweet what you love about the book with the hashtag #R2R and I'll do my best to connect with you.

Engage with me at:

Facebook: https://www.facebook.com/ryanblair.fans
Twitter: @RyanBlair
Instagram: @RyanViSalus
Sign up for our newsletter: ryanblair.com
E-mail me: r2r@ryanblair.com

Tell us your rock bottom to rock star story. In addition, we've created a series of short interviews called the "Rock Star Interviews" to illustrate and support the core lessons from the book. We gave entrepreneurs from all over the world, celebrities, and other successful people the same set of questions, revealing to us how they hit bottom and used their failure to create success. We want to hear your story, too. Go to: rockbottomtorockstar .com and take the Rock Star Interview quiz.

INDEX

INDEX

INDEX

INDEX

INDEX

INDEX